A MEMOIR OF SPIRITUAL LONGING
IN SECULAR LIFE

Winnowing

KIRA HIGGS

To true teachers and healers

and their willing students

TABLE OF CONTENTS

PREFACE

WORDS OFTEN ARE elusive when it comes to matters of the spirit. Perhaps it's best that way. Trying to describe spiritual inspiration or encounters with the divine tends to diminish them. Some even say that a mystical experience, by definition, defies description.

I don't disagree.

At the same time, I think we would do well to try to talk more about it. To listen to more voices—not just those of the anointed, the scholars, and the spiritual celebrities with book deals and massive social media followings, but also those of ordinary people on a path, making their way, discovering mysteries of who they are, gaining glimpses of the cosmos across the moments of their life. The more that people of different cultures, different countries, and different spiritual traditions speak up about their personal and shared experiences, the more we all stand to learn from the living spiritual traditions that blanket the earth. Especially if we can discuss our experiences with words that guide us into the same tent rather than segregate and separate. We're in need of voices that can build bridges and help us understand how we each taste and feel the world.

When I started writing a book in the summer of 2020, I

didn't have all this in mind. The world was four months into a pandemic. My husband and I were following instructions from our governor in Washington state. We were sheltering in place. My husband was antsy and eager to get on with a trip to Japan so he could officially launch his retirement travel. My work as an independent consultant had slowed. I figured I'd take advantage of the pause in the economy to enjoy quiet desk time. I was an experienced writer, having published articles, Op-Eds, and blog posts, and I looked forward to the new challenge of creating a book. I'd take a run at describing the techniques I used with organizational clients to unlock ideas and develop strategy. So, I began writing.

On day two, the wind blew out of the sails. This was not the book that wanted to be written. I sat at the computer surrounded by abject silence. Penning a business book had seemed like such a natural next step. By mapping my methods, I'd have something to share with up-and-coming leaders who couldn't afford to hire me. Virtually anyone would be able to access the gems of my personal knowledge base.

This book wanted to be something quite different. Disguised as prose, it quickly evolved into an offering, an ode to the spiritual tradition I consider my true home. The point of writing wasn't complicated. The guidance was clear.

Talk about your spiritual journey.

Reveal how you traversed chasms, by choice, not waiting for calamity to strike.

Include others—the sages and contemporary journeyers—who know a thing or two about entering the unknown.

Focus on a tiny audience. People who dare. Who thrive on the fire of aspiration and the voltage of higher realms.

Don't write about seeking.

Share the story of what it's like to find what you sought.

Offer them the gold.

INTRODUCTION

The day I realized I couldn't trust my own thinking, I was riding the Metro-North from Grand Central Station. I'd finished up another long day surrounded by other ambitious young investment bankers. We were the chosen ones—freshly minted college graduates who'd landed positions at the fourth-largest bank in the nation. I could analyze spreadsheets, construct financial packages. But original thought? That was another matter. The truth hit hard—not prompted by anything I could name, just suddenly present, fully formed: I could echo intelligence, but I wasn't able to generate it. I was twenty-five years old and already soured on the industry. As the express train flashed past each station, the platforms becoming a blur of space and speed, I wondered how one learns to truly think, to see beyond the obvious, to navigate by one's own light.

Variations of that question stayed with me for years. The answers weren't quick or easy, and some took decades to resolve.

I live my life linearly, as we all do. Today follows yesterday and tomorrow comes up next. Routines give a loose shape to the days, weeks and months. I follow a work schedule, sit down for meals, clean house, enact bedtime rituals, honor holidays and set off on vacations. The very living of life has made me who I am today.

At the same time, as I look back, I see the early signs of who I could become. Not a preordained destiny, but the seeds of possibility. Some seeds eventually blossomed into being. The student who cherishes learning. The craftsperson who loves to create. The athlete who can't go three days without exercise. The seeker who is grateful to teachers and mentors who encouraged autonomy, freedom, and trust in my own compass.

In penning the stories in this book, it's been both pleasure and challenge to recount black-and-white facts as best as I can while coloring around the edges to reveal something of the mysteries contained within those moments. Every event I write about made an impression, chiseled my consciousness in some way. Rarely, though, did I appreciate its impact when it occurred. Much of what happened made sense to me only later. I've discovered the beauty in exposing the fallacy of many of my first impressions. A second—or third or fourth—look revealed more truth and helped me see things to which I was too close to comprehend in the moment. It seems uncanny how, over an arc of time, many seemingly unrelated events contributed to learning and changing toward a single end.

What I know is that I've tried to operate with as much consciousness as I can muster at every stage of my life. Sometimes, I do it well. Often, I come up short. Striving for intellectual honesty isn't the same as being intellectually honest. The same goes for sensitivity to myself and others. Fortunately, my capabilities improved with time. Gradually, I developed navigational skills I could trust.

And that's the point of this book. I'm living proof that staying true to a genuine aspiration can go a long, long way toward reaching it. Aside from perseverance and curiosity, the key for me was staying open to the unknown, and the unwelcome. Which wasn't natural or easy. Distractions confounded me and confrontations with hard truths were discouraging. Cooking in spiritual fire involves an undoing that can be neither planned nor predicted. Still, the ultimate choice regarding how I navigate my life is mine.

Even though I've lived day after day in typical linear fashion, this book doesn't follow that sequence. It is organized around themes, so that stories from different times in my life can live together under a section heading. This also mimics how I learn; more like progressive peeling of onion layers than a one-hundred-meter dash or a transatlantic journey. Those are straight by comparison. The way it worked for me is that lessons returned. They deepened. Understanding became nuanced. What I held on to in early years eventually became easy to let go of. There were phases of building and dissolving, dissolving and building. Learning to navigate was as much about shaping my consciousness as it was about letting parts of it dissolve. And the process, taken as a whole, was intermittently deliberate, ecstasy inducing, frustrating and surprising. Within my influence and outside my control. Guided and mysterious. Sometimes, answers arrived, casting important light on a question's very essence.

If you're a reader who likes to bounce around to different

sections of a book, you'll discover that each chapter largely stands on its own. If, on the other hand, you prefer reading front to back, you'll encounter several time jumps, both forward and in reverse. In other words, these pages won't convey you smoothly through linear time. The first section chronicles stories of early years, and so do some later chapters. Assuming a simple chronology might be helpful, the basic breakdown is this: I was born in North Carolina, raised in New Hampshire, attended college in Massachusetts, worked in New York City and Minneapolis, then moved to Oregon (Ashland and later Portland). There, that should do it.

Regarding the stories, everyone I could track down has seen the passages in which they are mentioned; they have provided comments that either affirmed my recollection or expanded it. Nevertheless, it is not a shared telling of a story. The sum total of the experiences I write about speaks to changes that were largely interior, though many had exterior ramifications.

As you read or listen, I hope the stories kindle or rekindle a desire deep inside to forge your own clear-eyed approach to, and embrace of, divine mysteries.

Part I
Early Years

What is this mind of mine?
Where is the truth in it?
Attar, The Conference of the Birds

WONDERING

first things first

At two and a half years old, galloping on my hobby-horse in the living room of our small apartment in Durham, North Carolina, I made a discovery that would shape the rest of my life: my parents had no idea what they were doing.

I told my mom about it. Not at the time, but decades later.

"When I rode the hobbyhorse, I watched what everyone was doing. Everything going on in the household. Eventually it dawned on me, you and Dad didn't have a clue how to be parents."

I wasn't poking at her. There was no criticism leveled. Just two simple matters of fact. One, that's what was going on. Two, it was noticed.

She chuckled, partly to herself but also with me.

"You recognized that then?" she asked.

"Yeah."

"Well, you were right."

She conceded this without guilt. It's just the way it was. My mom and I were in a state of being with each other where the truth, seen from a certain angle, could be funny. Especially since we knew the same could be said of any parent. It's a multiyear exercise in making it up as you go.

As a toddler, I didn't understand that. When I sized up the situation, it looked as if someone other than my parents would need to figure things out, otherwise we were all doomed—Dad, Mom, my older sister, and I.

The person to resolve it would have to be me. It would have to be. I couldn't see anyone else getting around to it or even wanting to deal with it. I'd have to figure out a lot of things to pull this off, though.

And so, a little girl who learned to climb orchard trees and swung upside down on jungle gyms, who dressed up in velvet hats and leather boots, took on the impossible task of creating order out of chaos.

The conclusion was inescapable: I had to get it together. Fill the gap at home. Set us all up for better things. A childhood impression crystallized into a belief that snowballed into a plan, if one could call it that. First, I had to learn; being smart was the key to making sense of worldly things. Second, I had to do things correctly and do them well. From there, I figured, everything would fall into place. Observe, learn, take action, be good. However vague my notions were, they absorbed me and played out in both the foreground and background of my life.

To be clear, stepping up didn't mean taking care of anyone.

While I doted on my dolls, cradling and carrying them every-where, the idea of looking after humans held no appeal. No. What I was after was quite specific: for everyone to be okay so I could exhale. When things felt settled, something deep in my nervous system would relax. I'd find tranquility. When I sensed disharmony around me, things would feel unfinished, teetering on the brink.

To me, everything seemed to depend on intelligence, strength and getting things right. (It never occurred to me to question who determined any of this.) My training ground was everywhere—the schools I attended, the athletic fields where I competed and, most importantly, our household, where my older sister served as my unwitting guide. Elizabeth was clever, dimpled and daring, quick with whatever caught her eye. She hadn't welcomed my arrival; there are stories of her, at age four, pushing newborn me off the couch and drain-ing water from my bathinette when Mom wasn't looking. But after a few reprimands, she grew to enjoy teaching me what she knew. I watched everything she did and learned, mirror-ing what worked, avoiding what didn't, and sometimes doing the exact opposite. Proximity to her gave me a barometer for interpreting, and interfacing with, the world.

Elizabeth blazed her own trail in her choice of toys, clothes, friends—everything. She had a bright clarity to her thinking, aware of obstacles but refusing to let them alter her course. Nothing could deter her. Except our father. Her free spirit grated on whatever repressed him: his mother who favored her daughter over him, his grandfather who underwrote his Duke education, his bridled grief over the son who was born after me and died three months later. Elizabeth's confidence, her independence, her ease in claiming liberties he couldn't imagine for himself—it all scraped against buried wounds. And as her father, he believed it was his duty to rein her in.

One weekend when Elizabeth was in sixth grade, Dad snapped over her bangs. The long, eye-grazing style was the fashion then, made iconic by Twiggy. He'd told her repeatedly to get her hair out of her eyes. Mom kept special hair scissors for such trims, but Elizabeth hadn't bothered. Finally, he issued an ultimatum: he'd cut them himself if she didn't take care of it. As she headed upstairs, I watched him leave the kitchen and return with scissors—not Mom's delicate pair, but dull household shears. He yelled for her to come down.

Oh no, he's going to do it.

When she didn't respond, his voice deepened, thundering through our house. "Get down here, now!"

"Please don't, don't!" I begged.

It took two more bellows before she descended from her third-floor bedroom. She stomped in, face flushed, jaw set. In that moment, with her clean brown hair framing her defiance, she looked beautiful to me. Self-possessed. Unflinching. Certain she'd done nothing wrong. I was in her camp, baffled by the math of his rage. How could bangs warrant what was to come?

He lowered himself onto the kitchen chair and motioned her forward. They faced each other, her blue eyes flaring. Snip. Snip. Snip. The scissors moved briskly across her forehead, leaving her bangs grotesquely short and uneven, barely an inch and a half below her hairline. She stood silent, steaming, outwardly overpowered but inwardly certain: he was wrong, not she.

I cried more than she did. The brutishness of turning bangs into punishment horrified me. After the last clip, he paused to look at her. Humiliation completed. "They don't look bad," he said. We all knew otherwise.

Hair grows back, but not overnight. His handiwork would be there tomorrow, blazed across her forehead at school. What sixth-grade girl wouldn't crumble under that weight?

It was just one instance of him objecting to who she was and who she wanted to be. He released his cruelty on her. Every time Dad tried to snuff something out of her, I took note.

Don't do what she just did. Be what he likes.

And so, I learned how to catalog his likes and motivations, molding myself to fit. That's how I whittled my way into becoming his favorite—a stroke of genius I figured out all by myself. No one had to show me how.

Good grades in school helped; my report cards usually were flooded with A's. By age ten, I could hold my own in a swimming pool and by twelve, I was a tennis phenom thanks to lessons and practice guided by my father. I took the sport as seriously as he did. Winning ribbons at swim meets and collecting trophies at tennis tournaments made me feel . . . significant.

Then came crafts; I stumbled into the quiet, personal pleasure of creating things. I could puzzle through instructions on how to knit, sew and cook and emerge with finished products: a crimson wool scarf, narrow on the end where I started my first knitting project, wide at the finish after I'd learned how to relax the stitch. A white macramé belt with brass belt loops that I paired with low-cut bell-bottoms. Jumpers and dresses and tops of various shapes and colors. And apple pies made from scratch. With the right tools and a good set of instructions, I could take loose materials—from fabric to food—and create an entirely new form. Time spent creating was a haven, a solitudinal endeavor in which I could sort out questions of measurement, color and mechanics and be intrigued by what came out the other end.

By the time I was twelve, I'd internalized a reliable, step-by-step method for creating. If someone, somewhere knew what they were doing, and had written down the steps, then I could follow them. If I did, things worked out okay. This held true whether I swung a racket, played the piano or squeezed a flour sifter. It was reassuring to know that if I did everything right—or very close to it—I would end up with a pretty good outcome.

I was shaping my world with the means I had. In the foreground, doing things I liked to do. In the background, building my arsenal of personal power. I was discovering that when I applied myself to learn the rules and techniques, new things came into form. The more I did, the more skills I gained—writing in script, reciting multiplication tables, smashing overheads, acing pop quizzes, creating meals and playing Chopin. With more practice, I improved. This gave me confidence; the results spoke for themselves.

Observe, learn, take action, be good. Repeat. Repeat. Repeat.

Joseph-P

I was born at the tail end of the boomer generation. As a young child, I mostly took the world in; I didn't talk until after I was two. My mother, worried something might be wrong, arranged an appointment with the pediatrician.

"She's fine," he said. It wasn't long afterward that my vocal abilities emerged.

My parents had been childhood sweethearts in Greenville, North Carolina. They eloped when he was nineteen and she was eighteen. After Dad served in the Air Force and Mom finished putting herself through college, they started a family. I was their second child, the quiet one to my dimpled and precocious sister, Elizabeth. We were two years apart. When she was five and I was three, the family moved north to Long Island, New York.

While my sister and I were growing up, my mother bore trusses of Southern decorum. Sundays meant church, in patent leather shoes. For holidays we ate in the formal dining room, the table set with crisp white linens, sterling silverware and fine china. Our clothes were always ironed. And sleepwear included proper pajamas and a bathrobe.

After Mom saw an advertisement for a sale at Macy's, she took us shopping. As accustomed as she was to the finer things in life, she could get by on a tight budget and liked providing for her daughters.

We drove thirty miles in the family's Chevrolet Bel Air from St. James to Roosevelt Field. Mom guided us to children's sleepwear as we made our way past mountains of women's and men's clothing. Elizabeth took little time picking out a fluffy bright-yellow robe that zipped up the front. I was captivated by something I saw on the next rack.

"I don't want any of them. I want this one." I pointed to a striped robe with a palette of autumn hues—olive green, rusted orange, mustard yellow—and a tie at the neckline for closure.

"Those aren't on sale," my mother explained. "We came to get you bathrobes on sale. Choose something you like from here."

Elizabeth was already wearing the one she'd picked out. It looked nice on her. I couldn't be bothered trying on any of the single-color robes.

"No," I said. "I want this one."

"Those are too expensive," she insisted. "But you can get any one you like from this rack."

I didn't care about the sale. There was only one bathrobe that mattered. I was fixated.

"But I want the Josef-P robe," I pleaded.

"The what?"

"The Josef-P robe," I said, emphasizing the style of the robe that had caught my eye.

Mom gave me a quizzical look while Elizabeth stood by, having wrapped up her half the shopping mission.

"Josef-P." Surely she'd understand as I repeated it.

"But these are pretty," she said. "Feel how soft they are. Just try one on." The more she attempted persuasion, the more resistant I became. I wouldn't budge. We were nearing a stand-off in the children's section of the department store, but she didn't know that yet.

I raised my voice to convey my very important point. "I don't want that! I want the Josef-P robe!"

"But we can't afford it." She kept on with reason. "We only came for the sale. So you need to choose from these." She motioned in Elizabeth's direction.

"No!" I stomped. Then I dropped to the floor, still kicking my feet. "I want the Josef-P robe! I want the Josef-P robe!" The loud chant drew the attention of nearby shoppers, which flustered my mother. She bent down to calm me. I carried on. Her expression was one of embarrassment. She was horrified people might think that she couldn't control her wild child, or worse, that she was mistreating us.

"All right, you can have the robe," she said. She would have done anything at that point to get me to quiet down.

We left Macy's with two bathrobes: one full price and one on sale. It wasn't until we got home that Mom learned why I called it what I did.

"Why is it a Josef-P robe?" Mom asked, while putting me to bed.

Wearing it, I looked directly at her. "Joseph had a coat of many colors," I said nonchalantly. Wasn't it obvious? We'd learned it in Sunday School, where our teachers read stories and occasionally turned the pages toward us to show us the large illustrations.

It took a moment for all the elements to click into place, and when they did, Mom smiled. As a grammar lover, she was impressed by what I'd done. I'd seen the letter p in Joseph's name, but my phonetic understanding was limited. Calling the letter out, tacking it on the end where it appeared, seemed logical, even proper.

I loved that robe. It was durable and never wore out despite overuse and countless wash-and-dry cycles. Thirty years later it was passed down to my nieces. Dollar for dollar, it turned out to be the more frugal choice after all.

prayers from the baseline

When I was twelve, on a humid Sunday evening with darkness descending, I found myself sending desperate prayers skyward from a tennis court in New Hampshire. It was a no-holds-barred affair. Winning was all that mattered. My rival, Sharon, and I frequently met in the finals of the state circuit, and when we did, the court—usually a well of joy and self-soothing for me—always mutated to a battlefield. Our matches brought out the worst in us. We refused to pay each other compliments for winning shots, and we criticized ourselves after every unforced error.

Sharon was pretty when she smiled. I saw her smile only off court, or at the end of a match if she won. On court, her demeanor was stern. She wore her long hair in a ponytail with bangs that fell slightly above her eyeglasses. She was fit and strong, and when she showed up at a tournament, she meant business.

We were similar in size. I, however, was tuckered out, using every thimbleful of energy to chase down her drives. I didn't yet know I was severely anemic. I was lobbing most of my returns to buy time so I could shuffle back to the center.

Just keep the ball in play, that's all I have to do, I told myself as Sharon's killer instinct and near-perfect forehand drove the ball left and right.

What kept me going was how much I despised losing. Seeing my name progress on the draw sheet all the way to the champion slot made me feel special. Unique. I'd earned somewhat of a celebrity status in my hometown by beating grown women when I was ten. Besides, quitting anything never came naturally, and when I wanted something, I usually figured out a way.

Given my pitiful physical state, it seemed ludicrous that I should pull ahead, but I did. If I kept it up, the match might soon be over. Having competed against Sharon many times, I knew the tide could turn on a dime. Desperate, I did the last thing I dreamed might help. I prayed.

Back then, I thought prayers were exclusively about asking for help—either to stave off bad things or to get good things. You could pray for safety and stuff you really wanted. No need to bother, though, if you could do it on your own. If you didn't stand much of a chance without a boost, then utter a prayer. If it was really important, do it solemnly, maybe even on your knees with your hands clasped and your chin tilted up.

I whispered earnestly before each serve. *Please let me win this point.*

With every point that went my way, relief. I loped to the baseline to serve and raised my wish up higher in the sky. *Please, I want to win, to beat Sharon.*

She made errors. I won points. Maybe this is working, I thought. *Please. I hurt so much and can't lift my legs. Let me win, so this can be over.*

Though raised Episcopalian, I wasn't god-believing. More like god-fearing, given all the horrible things spelled out in the Bible. On the court that day, I was simply desperate. Maybe an angel would look kindly and take pity, end my suffering and help me close out this excruciating match. I reasoned that it was a gamble with no downside. If it worked, great. If it didn't, no ill would come of it.

I ended up winning the match and the title. The ordeal was finished at last. Did it work? Did my prayers make any difference? I have no inkling. After all, my whispers weren't prayers so much as the pleas of a feeble girl whose ambition exceeded her stamina. I suspect any presence above or beside me paid me no mind; I was a flailing innocent.

I prayed because, well, that's what people did. I'd learned that much in church and from my mother. She had made us memorize a prayer we said every night at bedtime.

Now I lay me down to sleep, I pray the lord my soul to keep.

If I should die before I wake, I pray the lord my soul to take.

Presumably, there was someone or something listening, and they were entitled to be as capricious as they wanted.

On the tennis court that evening, I felt no tangible sense of anything above my head, where god and angels supposedly lived.

How does anyone know there's such a thing as angels, anyway?

That's a big question.

That night on the court, the answer mattered not one iota. Whatever form of help I could get, I wanted it. I was greedy that way. I'd steal any advantage short of cheating.

When I won, I wasn't exuberant. Merely relieved. With the bout over, I could stop torturing my body. And I could conveniently forget about the prayers. I never bothered giving thanks for a potential helping hand. Given that I'd run myself ragged and I'd hung in there to the bitter end, didn't the credit belong to me?

After my parents drove me home, I ate dinner, showered, and tucked into bed. I probably said my nighttime prayer out of pure habit. The next day, my new trophy was tucked in with the others. And any possible notion of who or what might be up there answering our calls got tucked away, too.

the girl who knew god

The bells of the St. Paul's School chapel tower ring every fifteen minutes, marking time like a metronome. The brick buildings, man-made lakes and groomed playing fields of the campus create a wonderland for the development of young bodies, minds and spirits.

I arrived as a freshman in 1973, two years after the school went co-ed. At thirteen, I excelled at exactly two things: tennis and math. It's probably a good thing I didn't know what I didn't know. Had I foreseen what the next four years would entail—the emotional toll exacted in the transition from a modest public school to a bastion of privilege and academic rigor—my attending would not have been a foregone conclusion.

The ethos of the school came to life through ritual and routine. Chapel at 8:00 a.m. Afterward, on the steps outside, the day's announcements were read. Then students and teachers walked or biked to classrooms. Classes were small, typically no more than fifteen students. Afternoon sports were mandatory, and there was time to shower before everyone convened for dinner, where students sat at assigned tables with teachers who guided the conversation. We did homework and socialized in the evening. Extracurricular activities—theater rehearsals, writing for the school paper, debating, etc.—were squeezed in around this schedule.

Within my first few days at St. Paul's, it was clear I was in over my head. The longest book I'd read was under one hundred pages, and now we were diving into Charles Dickens's *A Tale of Two Cities*. Roundtable discussions blew past my comprehension. I was equally unprepared for the social world I'd entered—a textbook illustration of preppy. Well-heeled families from New York and Connecticut outfitted their children in Brooks Brothers khakis, L.L.Bean duck boots, Lilly Pulitzer dresses and Fair Isle sweaters. These kids operated on a coded set of unspoken norms. I, by contrast, was a townie on a scholarship.

St. Paul's was only two miles from home, but socially, emotionally, and intellectually it was a world away. I'd always enjoyed challenges, but this was a whole new terrain of hard, combined with uncomfortable. My nervous system stayed in a constant state of frustration—no amount of effort seemed to improve things fast enough. What I lacked in entry-level preparation, though, I made up for with persistent, strategic problem-solving, as Miss Deane, my groupmaster, observed in her summary report to my parents: *The examination period unsettled [her] a bit, but she certainly took it seriously and came through commendably.* Only in Math, and in a humanities course where I discovered Carl Jung's archetypes, did things click naturally.

My pluck paid off with what would now translate to solid B's and C's, with the occasional A in math and art. When I returned in the fall, I was better acclimated. I knew the routine and what was expected. And the housing lottery smiled on me.

I drew a single room in Simpson, a stone building with paned casement windows overlooking the main paths. Finally, my nervous system had a nightly haven.

One of my dormmates was Julia. She fascinated me precisely because she was everything I wasn't. While I approached my studies as something to conquer, she moved through classwork with natural ease. I was all protective layers and emotional defenses, armor I'd been steadily accumulating. But Julia seemed to need no such protection. Her jovial laugh and unguarded heart revealed a way of being I hadn't known was possible. I couldn't imagine living so openly, but I was drawn to her unencumbered nature and the light she carried.

I was surprised to learn she was god-centered. But it wasn't a creed. For Julia, it was a deeply relational experience. Her inner certitude was beguiling, and I began to wonder if I could have that, too, and if it would transform my Sturm und Drang into the serenity she embodied.

Soon, I was spending my evenings in Julia's dorm room, sitting cross-legged on her floor, pursuing one essential question: How does anyone know for sure that god exists? I wasn't looking to debate. If I could see through her eyes, maybe god's existence would become as obvious to me as it was to her. Because for Julia, faith wasn't faith at all. It was knowing. As she described it, the point wasn't that nothing would go wrong in her life or that in the end everything would be okay. She didn't expect to be shielded. Rather, when things went wrong, she wasn't alone. She was supported. This she knew.

As weeks passed, I approached the question from every

angle I could imagine. Julia met each attempt with surprising wisdom for a fifteen-year-old, offering words I could understand and meaning I could follow. But following a logical thread toward a reasoned answer proved not to be enough. The tangibility she experienced remained stubbornly hers, not mine. Our conversations always circled back to the same place.

"But how do you know there's a god?" I would ask.

"I don't know how," she'd answer. "I just do."

Sometimes, the breakthrough felt a hair's breadth away. If not tonight, I'd think, perhaps tomorrow night. But when I finally grew weary of reaching for something that dangled just beyond my grasp, I dropped the pursuit. Ever gracious, Julia said we could hunker down to chat again anytime. We stayed friends but never redressed my existential question.

Those evenings with Julia and her unguarded heart gave me a valuable data point. Authentic faith existed, even if it wasn't mine to claim. I loved that Julia had an intimate relationship with the divine. Buddhists have a term I've come to hold dear: "causeless joy." It includes the idea of celebrating the happiness of others. I truly celebrated hers. Besides, if Julia, at such a young age, had her own answers, maybe I would too, one day.

It gave me a little hope as I moved forward and turned my attention back to classes and sports—pursuits where effort reliably led somewhere. The question of god would have to wait; my inability to answer it didn't diminish the life unfolding before me. Compartmentalizing gave the whole ball of wax time to simmer in the background as I got on with growing up.

unconfirmed

There's a reason they call them prep schools. I turned into a proper poster child for what's possible when someone with discipline and motivation is offered an immersive learning opportunity. My grades improved, and when it was time for me to apply to college, it wasn't outrageous to think I'd enter the Ivy League. I was accepted at Princeton and turned it down for Williams College. The academics at both were superb, but I'd be taught by professors at Williams, not teaching assistants. Moreover, when I made weekend visits to both campuses, I saw two different mindsets. The culture of Princeton engendered striving to be best-in-class. Williams students cared about each other's success, not just their own.

The college is in Williamstown, which is barely bigger than a village and nestled in the purple mountains of the Massachusetts Berkshires. It was a three-hour drive from home. My first-semester classes were a breeze compared to classes at St. Paul's. I had no trouble making the varsity tennis team. And in the dorms, I had a single room within a suite, which conveniently balanced my needs—to be alone and among others. My emotional undercurrent as a freshman in high school was panicked, whereas now I felt victorious.

But at this larger school with so many new faces and three hours from home, I felt lonely, a tinge of emptiness. I missed my family. I missed the morning ritual of coming together in chapel to ease into the day. I missed being held by something bigger than me.

I started going to the Episcopal church. It was a quaint stone building on the edge of campus. I was immediately taken in, welcomed, embraced by congregants who lived in and near the town. As there were no other college students in view, it felt like my private discovery. Sunday services weren't just familiar; they offered a warmth that passed through me like a balm. Almost every sermon spoke to something I'd wondered about—or should wonder about. By and large, they related to daily life and offered different ways to think about situations that I, too, found myself in. I grew more and more fond of the people, the moments together, and the lift it gave my spirit.

After I'd settled into a rhythm with academics, sports and part-time jobs to help cover tuition, something began niggling at me. Three years earlier, I'd stowed away a question I couldn't resolve: How does anyone know for sure that god exists? Going to church every week stirred the pot. I wasn't ambivalent about attending, only about the god thing. I enjoyed my time at the church so much that surely the question would sort itself out if I kept coming. I kept looking, sensing, feeling, angling for proof. The irony was that I'd been confirmed by the church when I was fourteen, but privately, at my core, I could find no confirmation.

Months went by. There was no progress in my thinking or perception. I still didn't know if there was a god. It never went so far as a definitive no—I wasn't an atheist—but I couldn't see or hear or feel an actual *there* there. I started to feel like a hypocrite. It was worse than uncomfortable. The discord stabbed at me.

If I didn't come clean to the minister about my beliefs, I'd be living a lie. I owed it to myself, and to the church, to be honest. After all, these were good people who were drawn together in community for worship and prayer. I, however, didn't attend because I believed in god and wanted to experience god in fellowship. I attended because the traditions and the camaraderie made me feel good. To admit this was to risk losing a place that nourished me emotionally, but I couldn't ignore how simple and obvious, how black-and-white the situation appeared—given I didn't believe, I shouldn't go anymore. Reciting Bible passages and prayers that weren't true for me felt awful. I learned much later that many churchgoers don't mind having ambiguity, and for some it's actually a reason to go. It's no problem. But to me it was excruciating.

I scheduled an appointment with the minister. I wanted to tell him my decision in person rather than write a letter.

We sat together in his office. He listened as I explained my dilemma. He asked questions. We had a straightforward and honest conversation. He wanted me to know that there was no issue—I could attend even if I was unsure. He didn't think of me as a hypocrite; only I did. There was plenty of room in his mind and heart for me to be in whatever phase of discovery—including reaction or rebellion—I was in. I wasn't alone in my ambivalence about god's existence.

But none of that felt right. The way to resolve the discordance inside was to stop saying things I couldn't stand behind. Instead of attending services and not speaking while those around me recited the liturgy, I needed to leave.

For the sake of integrity, I quit, knowing I'd grieve the loss of the people, the emotional support, the community, the ritual. The minister said that he respected me for doing what I felt was right, and that the door was always open. Julia had said the same.

I quietly departed after saying goodbye to church friends on my last Sunday. I told them why I needed to go. They neither judged nor tried to convince. They simply hugged me and said they hoped I'd be back. I did, too. Nothing would make me happier than to return on newly formed solid ground, with the answer to my question giving way to confidence in genuine knowing.

For the next three and a half years, each time I passed the chapel I felt a little tug, but not regret. Having been true to my inner compass, I could live with myself and the pain. I graduated from college without ever re-entering the church.

DISCOVERING

get it

When I went home for spring break during my junior year at Williams, I found that Mom and Dad had turned into people I didn't recognize. The Southern accents were still there, as was their humor. But a cloud had lifted, and the cultural tendency they grew up with—skating around uncomfortable conversations—had been replaced by something electric and direct. They'd done est—Erhard Seminars Training—on the recommendation of Dad's favorite colleague. Now, they spoke with an aliveness that cut through bullshit. Conversations started and ended with precision. Their words had edges. Their eyes were clearer. Even their physicality seemed different, their bodies more present, more awake. To many, this change might have been repellent, but I found it magnetizing. It set a stage for surprising connections. For the first time, I felt us meeting eye to eye with the freshness of moment-by-moment truth rather than the rote of habit.

Convinced it would improve our lives, Dad leaned on my older sister and me to follow suit. That summer, we drove together to Boston for two consecutive weekends to take the est training. Hour after hour, we sat in straight-backed hotel chairs while students rose one by one, gripped the microphone, and poured out their troubles. The stories blurred together: neglectful parents, bad bosses, uncaring spouses, rotten children. Always someone else to blame. While other students nodded, gasped, and wiped away tears, I shifted restlessly in my chair, wondering why these people couldn't just fix their problems and move on.

The trainer had her work cut out for her. A tall woman in her thirties or early forties with eyes that both sparkled and pierced, she stalked the stage like a lioness, tearing into each person's story with ruthless precision. When someone couldn't grasp her point, she'd descend from the stage in swift strides and thrust her face inches from theirs, sometimes screaming to break through their defenses. Oh no, I thought, watching her rip another participant's reality to shreds. This can't be the same seminar that transformed my parents.

I spent most of those sixty hours trying to learn from this madness, wanting to follow the point but never grokking it. The room crackled with breakthrough moments and emotional releases. At nineteen, I couldn't relate to these middle-aged people sobbing about their divorces and dead-end careers. I lacked the life experience to understand their pain, let alone their revelations.

When the final crescendo came—the big cosmic joke that had everyone else laughing in recognition—I sat dumbfounded. "Did you get it? I got it!" students called to each other across the room. I got nothing except confirmation that adults could hurt for unnecessary reasons, and the useful discovery that I could stay awake all night when needed, a skill that would serve me well during senior-year all-nighters.

For me, tectonic shifts usually follow a slow burn. That was certainly the case with est. I had no earth-shattering breakthrough in the training. During my senior year at Williams, however, something stewed in the background. "The truth will set you free, but first it will piss you off." These words, spoken during those sixty hours in Boston, kept nagging at me. I don't recall exactly when the switch flipped, but once it did, est became my gospel.

After graduation, I landed in New York, a major hub in the national est network, and fell headlong into the movement. I became someone known as an est-hole, signing up for every seminar I could afford, evangelizing to friends and colleagues about the flagship course, and volunteering on evenings and weekends at headquarters and events.

For a long stretch, I served as doorkeeper for est graduate seminars. The job came with explicit directions. When the instructor began speaking—always exactly on time—I closed the door. Period. Any late arrivals faced me and my series of predetermined questions. They couldn't enter until I "cleared" them, one at a time, even if they arrived with others. I guarded a threshold that was precious to est followers: the chance to transform their lives. To cross it, they had to confront a tension between the world of ordinary excuses and the basic principles of accountability.

I started by telling them where to stand—directly in front of me. Eye to eye.

"Are you late?" I'd ask, in a neutral tone.

"Yes." Hard to argue with evidence. The meeting room door was shut, and it never closed prematurely.

"Did you agree to be on time?" Question number two.

"Yes." Again, hard to argue. When registering for a seminar, everyone signed an agreement. Among other things, it stipulated arriving on time.

"Did you break your agreement?" The discomfort usually began here. Emotional squirming. Often, a story about traffic. Last-minute snafus at work. A sick kid.

"Did you break your agreement?" It was my job to repeat the question in the same tone. Never engage, agree, dispute, or teach. If a conversation started up because the student wanted to explain, it was a one-way dialogue. I returned to the question over and over until they simply said yes.

"Yes." Eventually nearly everyone got there.

Out of the dozens of late students I cleared, only one ever turned and left the building.

Up to this point in the exchange, people often pushed against me. Not physically, but through body language, glares, sharpness of words. Sometimes they sprinted down the hall, hoping to slip through the door before the latch fastened. Blocked from entering, they turned me into their adversary. I was the one thing standing between them and the conference they'd paid for.

"Are you responsible for breaking your agreement?"

This is usually when their edge started to recede. Their neurology was adjusting. The blaming stopped; their gestures were calmer. Being forced to acknowledge that it was all on them, their brains caught up with reality. I wasn't the bad guy. They were just . . . late. After promising to be on time.

At this point, they were quick to answer.

"Yes."

"Do you agree to recommit?"

"Yes." Hastily delivered.

The worst of the grilling behind them, they now wanted to get in the room. Most seminar leaders were charismatic. People liked learning from them and didn't want to miss a word.

"Will you keep your commitment?"

"Yes."

"Thank you. You're cleared."

I'd open the door a crack to peek in and see if the seminar leader was accepting late arrivals. As soon as I saw the signal, I'd permit the student to pass. They'd slide inside and look for an open seat.

From time to time, a student approached me after class to apologize.

"I'm sorry I was so rude to you. Thanks for staying with me."

It wasn't an easy or comfortable volunteer assignment. I didn't like playing a hard-ass, even a neutral one. Standing erect, looking up into the eyes of taller people (usually men) who were pissed off and projecting their anger on me wasn't my idea of a good time. I chose the role as a stretch. To challenge a personal limit.

After a few months of the drill, I was proficient. I could hold my own without worrying I'd buckle under the pressure of someone's ire. And with that came a sense of confidence that I could stand up, adult to adult, when someone wanted to wring my neck.

Eventually the whole family did est. My younger siblings flew to Northern California for the teen version. The family dynamic that emerged was more to my liking. I can get the score when people are straight, and when they're not, I end up investing energy I don't want to spend trying to understand what's going on. Our communication was jargon-heavy at first, and that was okay. It reinforced changes we wanted to make. Later, our language returned to normal, but many effects of the training were long-lived. For us, it was no flash in the pan.

Whether I fell too deep into est or got out too soon, its core principles—integrity, truth, keeping one's word—rewired my brain. Werner promised that this rigor would lead to creative possibility, with a stronger sense of agency in life. Through countless hours in seminars and serving as assistant to the assistant director in New York, I'd learned to take radical responsibility for my life. It was indeed freeing, just as Werner proclaimed. But freedom, I was discovering, came with its own existential challenge: What, exactly, did I want to choose?

the reading

The career counselor at the NYU business school had tried everything. Aptitude tests. Personality assessments. Informational interviews with alumni. Now, over lunch at a restaurant near campus, Marian—my assigned counselor and the model of professionalism—was suggesting something radical.

"Here's the name of someone I think you should meet," she said, sliding a slip of paper across the table.

I expected another executive's contact. Instead, Marian had written one name: Vivian. Below that, Vivian's number.

"Vivian is a psychic. And a singer. In fact, I think she's currently on Broadway in a show with Raul Julia."

I must have scrunched my face in a quizzical look, because Marian quickly added, "Don't worry, she's not weird. She's usually spot-on. She's helped several of my clients learn important things about themselves when traditional career counseling didn't work."

"You've sent other people to her?"

"Yes, but just a few. Usually, the work I do with clients gets the job done. But sometimes there's a block, something in the way of knowing what they want. Vivian gets to the bottom of it. She's good."

Good or not, I'd never been curious about or interested in psychics. I assumed they were charlatans.

I'd been exposed to new everything since leaving New England for New York City. I dressed differently. I carried myself differently. I moved in different circles. But now that I was inside the financial industry, the luster had dimmed. Despite the sense of so much possibility, I didn't know which way to turn. Career was the most important part of my life, but I felt directionless.

Like most bankers, I'd enrolled in an MBA program—night classes at NYU, as my employer offered tuition reimbursement for these particular classes. That's how I found Marian. The career counseling office paired me with her, and for months she'd thrown everything in her toolkit at my indecision, to no avail. If Vivian couldn't give me answers, I'd be out only seventy-five dollars. I called to schedule.

Vivian saw clients in her Midtown apartment. She buzzed me into the building, and I went to the fifth floor, where her door was slightly ajar. I expected a woman in a full-length cape and pointy wizard hat. Instead, Vivian wore loose gray sweats. As soon as we sat across from each other in the living room, she suggested I pay up front. "People often forget afterward." I wrote the check and handed it to her.

She settled into a chair with a can of Diet Coke and her

cat nearby. Then she put a blank cassette in a handheld tape recorder and set it on the coffee table between us.

"Testing testing testing."

She went silent for a moment before talking. The next hour blew my mind.

It was as if she were reading my biography. Her descriptions of my upbringing and my challenges were startlingly accurate. She didn't speak in universal terms—she was quite specific. Some parents recognize their children's proclivities and mirror their gifts back to them. It's a form of witnessing that allows the child to cognize something of their essential nature. My parents did that to a large degree, but Vivian's insights defined features of my personality that no one ever had, and that I had missed. Almost everything she said was uncannily accurate.

She asked to look at my palms.

"This [left] hand can get devastated. This [right] hand bounces back." Everyone knew I was resilient. As for the tender bits, I kept them hidden. They were the most dangerous part of me; they could get me hurt. I concealed moments of devastation so well that people had no idea. From there, her comments became even more personal.

"Your teenage years were pretty revolting. But you've managed to come out of that quicker than most people have." Quite plausible. I'd survived the pressure cooker of boarding school and emerged with more confidence. I wanted to get on with life as an adult, and that's what I was doing.

"You have an incurable romanticism that's deadly." Zing. Ever the practical one, I had another side that held a profound belief in love as a perfect union, both noble and attainable. The ideal had taken on a life all its own.

"Your expectations in people are seldom met." I hated hearing this. It hit a raw nerve because I expected a lot of others. It was doubly worse with boyfriends, given my fantasy of how love should go.

These two traits in particular would complicate my life for decades to come.

I didn't, however, get a definitive answer about what to do in my career. Quite the opposite.

"You have an eye for color and a sense of form."

"As successful as you will be in business, it won't make you happy."

"You can do anything you put your mind to. And our guides say your spiritual development is more important than what you do."

Well, that certainly didn't narrow things down.

Vivian held back advising me, save one important slice that has stuck with me in the years since. In sharing it, she opened a door I didn't know was closed.

"You think you have to earn money in order to have the things you want," she said. "It's much smarter to wish for the things you want rather than the means to acquire them. It's faster to just get them."

So true.

"Focus on what you want. How it manifests might surprise you. Maybe it will be given to you. Maybe someone will say, 'Turn here,' and it takes you where you want to go."

"And sometimes," she added, "the detour turns out to be the shortest path."

Seventy minutes later, I left Vivian's apartment. I had a cassette recording of the session in my purse and a list of far-flung destinations that could awaken me. They were all in Asia. I never went to a single one.

I'd booked with Vivian for a career reveal and, in a strict sense, I didn't get what I paid for. Instead, she'd lightheartedly dropped a stick of dynamite into my worldview. For the first time, it seemed conceivable to me that people could know things without prior knowledge. Moreover, I clearly didn't know myself as well as I'd thought I did. Her characterizations were accurate but unbeknownst to me until she named them.

Another Vivian, the supervisor at my campus job in college, wrote a beautiful card when I graduated. *The world is your oyster.* She sincerely meant it. On this, the two Vivians agreed. Their belief in my limitless potential was genuine.

What I hadn't yet learned was that what I want will never be fixed and settled. It changes and evolves as I do. And the things I want the most—deep deep down inside—will always be announced softly. Never with a trumpet or a firecracker.

I want to buffer pain for my father as he succumbs to cancer.

I want my husband to know, and cherish, the most delicate facets of my inner being.

I want to be at ease conversing in Spanish.

I want the people I adore to know they are showered in love.

A new proposition started taking shape after seeing Vivian. It was simultaneously scary and exciting because the rules of life I'd acquired and constructed were too limiting. Maybe there was more than one way to eat an oyster.

walk with me

Every evening for months, I held myself together on the Metro-North train from Grand Central Station to Greenwich. After I climbed two sets of stairs to my in-law unit above Mr. and Mrs. Conti's modest home and entered my small apartment, the tears flowed as if on cue. By day, I was an up-and-coming young banker in a suit, navigating deals in Midtown Manhattan. By night, I was a wreck—a heart-broken twenty-five-year-old whose joyous plans had shattered.

The breakup blindsided me. After two years with Jay, marriage felt inevitable. We were discovering New York together, our infatuation growing with each weekend adventure. I thought I'd done most things, if not everything, right since leaving my small town for New York City: land the banking job, master squash, attend the right personal development seminars. When we moved in together in his Queens row house, it seemed like the natural next step.

Then everything unraveled. I had mistakenly assumed the way to deepen our bond was to be more of who I thought he wanted me to be. I stifled my preferences to accommo-date his, and in the process turned into someone neither of us recognized. He withdrew and then told me to leave.

Having made what I presumed were sensible sacrifices, I was stunned.

I found a place north of the city, far enough removed from the skyscrapers and metal canyons, and saw Jay only twice afterward. My new routine was simple: crunch numbers by day, cry at night, read before bed, and during lunch breaks, peruse the shelves of the Theosophical Society bookstore. I imposed a strict rule. For one year, no advice from friends or family. Especially from Dad, whose fatherly concern for his flock often was doled out as instructions—the best thing to do or the right way to do it. Anyone else's wisdom, however well-meaning, would impede the development of my judgment. I needed to learn to think for myself.

I turned to Theosophical sages. When I read what they wrote, I was temporarily lifted above my circumstances. Their thinking rankled, in a good way, the twentieth-century baggage I carried in my head. With perseverance and a little luck, I'd extract the answer to how a love that felt so real could evaporate in an instant.

A few months after the split, I called Loni, a friend who worked at the bank and took est graduate seminars. We arranged to meet for lunch at the company's upscale cafeteria.

"I still don't understand how it happened," I said, keeping my voice low so coworkers at the next table couldn't hear. She was both sympathetic and practical, asking if it was truly over (yes, he wouldn't return my calls) and whether I'd done all I could (I had).

She surprised me when she pivoted to an unrelated topic.

"I've been exploring new things lately," she said. "I heard about channeling and decided I wanted to try it out. It was wild!"

"What do you mean channeling?" I asked. I pictured monster-size equipment boring holes through bedrock to build underwater freeways.

"There are people who are aware of things at frequencies other people don't notice," she said. "I guess they hear voices, and channel them. I thought it was weird, but I was curious so I went to a session with one of them. It shocked me how much insight came of it."

I still neither believed nor didn't believe in god, but the idea sounded as if it were on the far extreme on the spectrum of belief. My skepticism felt edgy and cold, abjectly inconvincible. At the same time, I was seeking answers. I consumed Western esoteric texts that spoke of living knowledge and worlds unseen. How bad could channeling be?

"How does it work, exactly?"

"Rhea is her name. I'm not sure how it works. The night I went, there were twelve of us in her living room. We sat on the floor in a circle, with Rhea in the middle. She gave us instructions, then lay down on the rug. Everyone got to ask one question. Rhea said she gets out of the way and lets the Archangel Michael speak through her. He's the one listening and answering, not her. She said she doesn't remember her words afterward."

"How personal were the questions everyone asked?"

"Very. Like, really. The night I went someone asked about whether to get a divorce."

"What did you ask about?"

"I've been on the fence about changing jobs. I'm bored and don't see a promotion in the cards anytime soon."

"What did you learn?"

"That in three months, it will be clear what to do."

"Does that sound right to you?"

"I'll have to wait and see. But I know I'm not as anxious now."

"Do you really think it's the Archangel Michael?"

She leaned back and sighed. "Well, why don't you see for yourself?"

I'd always admired Loni's practicality and levelheadedness. I supposed it couldn't hurt to try it.

&

It was a weeknight in early spring, still light when I took the subway to Times Square. The last to arrive, I hurried to stow my coat and briefcase in the bedroom before joining the others, who made space for me in the sitting circle on the floor. Loni wasn't there; she hadn't planned on attending.

We were an even number at ten. I appeared to be the youngest. We weren't invited to introduce ourselves, not even our first names, perhaps to preserve anonymity so people felt comfortable asking whatever they wanted and hearing whatever they were told.

After we settled into our cushions, Rhea, an attractive woman in her early forties wearing a plain shirt and loose slacks, welcomed us in a gentle voice. She explained how she'd discovered her ability to channel, and emphasized that she wasn't responsible for what the Archangel Michael said through her. As she lay down, brushing her long brown hair across her left shoulder, the room grew quiet. Her assistant, seated near her head, would facilitate, calling on people as they raised their hands. I watched and listened.

Over the next ninety minutes, people asked about jobs, money, relationships and dead relatives. Rhea's voice was deep, solemn and reassuringly calm—bearing little resemblance to her earlier tone. The answers themselves seemed to get to the heart of the questions with surgical precision, without oracular remarks or hopeful predictions. They offered understanding, not promise.

Finally, I raised my hand. Rhea's assistant signaled to me.

"I would like to know why my relationship ended." My voice was steady, polite, revealing nothing. This was my test: Could Rhea—or the Archangel Michael—truly know anything about my life?

The response was like a newspaper horoscope, vague and impersonal. Something about how some of the most valuable relationships are transitory, serving as prompts for self-development. Heat rose in my chest, along with months of suppressed anger and confusion. I blurted out, "Then why does it hurt so bad?!" It was a question and a plea.

The answer, Rhea-Michael said, had to do with past lives, one in particular where Jay was my father. I had a child out of wedlock. As punishment, he disowned me.

I'd never considered the plausibility of past lives. But as our two years together flashed through my awareness, the characterization seemed to fit perfectly. His righteousness, his swift withdrawal of affection, had felt deeply personal. Now, I saw it from a different angle, as part of a pattern larger than just us in this life, speaking more about him than me. In the broadest sense, we both played roles in the demise of our relationship. If past lives were any clue, we were predisposed to unravel. Something in my chest loosened at this new perspective, easing just a fraction of the ache.

Afterward, anxious to catch the last train home, I gathered my things and dashed out. The moment the elevator doors closed behind me, the air changed. Not in the usual way elevators shift pressure in your ears—this was entirely different. A force filled the small space, wrapping me in what felt like an invisible blanket of pure warmth and love. It was so tangible I could almost stroke it with my fingertips, as real as touching silk or wool.

Stepping out of the elevator, I expected the sensation to dissolve. Instead, the blanket stayed with me, its presence just as palpable on the dark, quiet street. As I walked toward Grand Central, I noticed something else: this presence cloaked me in protection. It wasn't just comfort—it actively ensured my safety. As a woman alone at night with a purse and briefcase in that part of town, I should have felt vulnerable. Instead, I knew with absolute certainty no harm would come. Only when I settled into my seat on the last commuter train did the blanket gradually fade.

⤸

I'd experienced intuition before. Coincidence. Serendipity. I'd felt my heart crack open during weddings and while singing in a choir. But this was entirely different. Something had immersed me in its presence, made itself known beyond doubt. If I'd relied only on my eyes, I wouldn't have believed it. But I felt it as surely as a hand resting on my arm.

I never gave this presence a name. Under the circumstances, it would have been easy to assume it was Archangel Michael. But since I had no relationship with him or any deity, why waste time with names? Instead, I wondered why this was happening. This something that I didn't know from past experience: Did it know me? How did I get on its radar? I had a slew of questions that would find no answer.

What I do know is this. I didn't care that no one was with me to validate it. It was as bona fide as the sun. It had an intelligence very different from my own. It knew what it was doing. It didn't ask anything of me. It simply accompanied me, transferring wordless guidance on how to not push it away. How to hold myself during our fleeting magical interface. How to quiet my mind and maintain the silence inside while being visited by divinity.

It didn't make a total believer out of me. That spring evening didn't erase all skepticism. But it went a long way. I couldn't deny that it had happened. And that my ability to feel and perceive something invisible was real, too.

the crux

Even when I take vacation, I need to design little projects to keep me from getting antsy. This combination of industriousness, honesty and smarts made me a pretty good employee, but past a certain point, the question became "What do I want to do?"

I liked the challenge of my work in banking for the first few years. The income was great, and I enjoyed most of the people. But I yearned to make more of a difference.

Neither career counseling nor my sit-down with a psychic had hinted at what direction to pursue. One day, I remembered a Christmas visit to a local nursing home over college break. My family aimed to uplift the residents with the carols we sang, but the sight of wheelchairs filled with listless elders staring into space and alone during the holidays sent shock waves through my heart. I fled to the stairwell and hid, choking back tears, hoping my visible distress hadn't compounded theirs. That memory haunted me. I wondered about the models in our country for long-term care and, by extension, hospitals. The whole system of healthcare and eldercare appeared broken, ripe for transformation. I figured this might be where I could apply myself.

I researched, and I spoke with alumni in my college network who confirmed my hunch that leading change in that industry would be challenging—so much was dysfunctional, in need of change—but the upside potential and personal reward could be huge.

My résumé was a problem; I didn't have an ounce of experience in that field. One alum recommended getting a health practitioner license, and from there, a graduate degree in administration. I rejected the idea of such a long, arduous route and instead calculated the fastest path—I'd request a lateral transfer to the healthcare finance division.

When I put in for the transfer, my senior vice president called me directly. He wanted to meet.

The appointment was at his office. He motioned for me to sit in the leather chair facing his large walnut desk. His manner was, as always, bright and alert.

"I'll give you the transfer," Dick said.

"Thank you! That's wonderful!"

"On one condition."

I was listening.

"I'm putting together a special team to work on a new product. If you commit to one year, I'll sign the transfer."

A lot of buttering up on his part ensued. Great contributor.

Go-get-'em attitude. Good energy. Innovative program. Needs a strong team.

"Well, can I think about it?" I asked.

"Of course. Let me know."

One year later, after I'd put in my time on his new team, I was back in Dick's office.

"You've done great work. I'd like to ask you to stay another year."

Are you kidding me?

"No, you said one year," I reminded him, thinking he might have forgotten.

"I expected that would be your answer, but I had to try. I gave you my word and I'm keeping it. I do hate to lose you."

Dick signed the paperwork and said that any time I wanted a job in his division, he'd have one for me.

My first project in the new department involved approving a simple line of credit for a national blood supplier. Straightforward, usually. Not this time. HIV/AIDS had just come into the news. People were dying. The Centers for Disease Control didn't understand the disease and how it was transmitted.

Banks make money on calculated risk. This transaction was a hard risk to calculate. I was too green behind the ears to register the full implication for blood banks.

Joseph, a wise-cracking municipal analyst with the prized corner desk, lent me a hand. He always cut through the haze, whether it was about structuring deals or mapping the undercurrents of office politics. I showed him my analysis before it went upstairs to the executive team for review and approval. If I wrote it well, I wouldn't have to defend it in person.

"There's one question that's key, you know," he said, matter-of-factly.

I didn't know.

"What are you thinking of?" I asked.

"What happens if the supplier ends up with tainted blood?"

Tainted blood. That was the crux.

In banking, the point isn't to eliminate all risk. Banks wouldn't make any money that way. It's to recognize the nature of the risk and the price of it. Joseph put his finger on it.

I edited my proposal and submitted the paperwork; it came back approved.

Joseph saw what was hiding in plain sight. Whether he cared one way or the other was irrelevant. He simply saw it and named it. He made the invisible visible.

I wanted to be able to do that.

a thousand angels

After five years, the bloom was off the rose in New York City. I craved nature. I'd shifted my focus to health-care finance, had a great salary and benefits and did good work. Using money to make more money, however, left me flat at the end of the day. I needed another change—away from finance and toward administration. I learned that two urban centers were already upending the shape of the industry. That was where I'd go and what I'd do.

I chose Minneapolis over Raleigh-Durham-Chapel Hill. I loved the big sky and predicted I'd tolerate its bitingly cold winters better than the protracted humidity and racism of the South. Through a friend of a friend, a connection materialized at a midsize healthcare system. The timing and fit were perfect—they needed someone who understood finance and could learn marketing for a newly designed role. A month after accepting their offer, I was settling into an apartment three times the size of my New York rentals at a fraction of the cost.

Things fell easily into place. My new boss was a visionary. My colleagues welcomed me with Midwestern kindness.

Even Minnesota's notorious weather seemed to smile on me, greeting me with sunny autumn days perfect for exploring the lakes and bike trails of my new neighborhood. After years of striving in New York, this course correction of home and career felt . . . right.

A month after moving, I returned home one day to my apartment on Xerxes Avenue. Everything looked normal—my furniture exactly where I'd left it, windows still closed, nothing out of place. Yet the moment I stepped inside, I knew something was radically different. It wasn't the temperature or humidity, nor was it a scent. It was . . . the fullness of a soft, powerful and tangible presence. Whatever it was, it didn't feel as if it was of this world, at least not as I had come to know physical reality. It was invisible yet so present I could almost feel its weight in the air. Inviting, caressing. This was my home, yet something else was here, extending itself and welcoming me into the living room.

It reminded me of the experience I had after meeting Rhea-Michael—of that invisible presence that wrapped around me, blanketing me in warmth, protection and infinite caring. Similarly, this defied words. The difference was that whatever was in my living room wasn't a single thing. It was a multitude packed to the gills. Standing room only.

Well, I thought, maybe the reason is to encourage me to meditate for a few minutes.

I was neither well-versed nor well-practiced in meditation—far from it. I'd had a single introduction to meditation when a friend invited me to an evening with seasoned practitioners of Gurumayi. Their chanting transported me to blissful serenity and a sensory experience of stillness and inner silence I'd never felt before. It was glorious. I bought the recording of Gurumayi's mantra and tried it at home, but my monkey mind wouldn't stop spinning through to-do lists, recent conversations and other silly distractions. Absent regularity or any deep satisfaction, I still limped along.

I settled cross-legged on the couch and closed my eyes. My mind seemed quieter than usual, but nothing revelatory happened. After twenty-five minutes, I opened my eyes. The presence remained, but my interest waned. I moved on with my evening routine of dinner, chores, and reading in bed until sleep came. I slept like a rock.

The next morning dawned ordinary—shower, breakfast, dishes. Then I stepped outside, and my world tilted on its axis. The shared garage was a blackened skeleton; all but the cinder-block walls had burned to a crisp. My car was an unrecognizable heap of melted metal. The acrid smell of ash hung thick in the air.

I darted back inside to call 911.

"I need to report a fire!" I blurted, as soon as the dispatcher answered.

"What is your address, ma'am?"

I told her.

"Just a moment." A short pause before she spoke. "We show there was a four-alarm fire there last night."

"You already knew there was a fire?" I asked, stunned.

"Yes, it was called in at 2:02 a.m."

"Why didn't any trucks come?" I asked.

"Ma'am, our records show four trucks at the scene." Impossible. She had to be mistaken.

"Are you positive? I didn't hear them. Did they sound their alarm?"

"Yes, ma'am. Full sirens, four-alarm fire."

"I don't understand."

Dazed and confused, I pressed the dispatcher with more questions. Was she absolutely sure? I was there last night. I didn't hear or see a fire or emergency vehicles. Was I in the twilight zone?

Slowly, slowly the reality sank in. I'd slept through the commotion. The blaze was twenty feet from my bedroom window. I never heard a thing.

Later, news came out that this was part of a series of fires, an arsonist's rampage through the city that had been going on for weeks. One of the tenants probably didn't close the garage door all the way, so the latch didn't catch. Or they forgot to turn the lock. When the insurance adjuster came later that day to inspect my car, he asked what brand it was. No visual hints remained.

My next call that morning was to the office to say I'd be late. They were as concerned as could be. Though it wasn't their fault, they felt guilty. The woman they'd recruited and helped get established in her new home had been victimized there.

I, however, was grateful, once I got over the shock. A car is just a car. Relatively easy to replace. But life is precious. That night, mine was spared. It would have been easy enough for sparks to float from the garage and land on the roof of the apartments. One fire could have been two. Everyone else in my building and dozens of folks living nearby woke up and witnessed the event. But I'd been in a deep slumber. I could have died in my sleep.

Then, I put two and two together. I had been blanketed by something otherworldly. Again. This time a term for it floated through my mind: a thousand angels. They'd assembled not to entice me to meditate but in anticipation of what was to come. They'd arrived hours before the first match was lit.

If I'd never noticed this packed house of celestial beings, I might never have known their part in the story. It was a direct experience, unmistakable and irrefutable. It helped me to finally answer the question I'd been carrying since I was a teenager.

How does anyone know for sure that god exists?

I had my answer.

Through direct experience. Nothing replaces such a moment, and nothing can take it away.

I was never good at pretending, which is why I couldn't trust the liturgy, take anyone's word about god or fake it till

I made it. I had my evidence, earned firsthand rather than through borrowed faith. I'd wondered, waited, watched and finally seen. I arrived where I arrived without guesswork, wishful thinking, or blind acceptance. Just aspiration to have a particular question answered.

Now, I knew what I knew, which, to be frank, didn't feel like a whole lot. Just a kernel with atomic-size relief. I no longer had to wonder about the existence of the divine. I was on solid ground having arrived honestly at my conclusion.

But the mysteries of existence, by contrast, hadn't diminished. If anything, they'd expanded. There was so much learning to come.

harmony

The first time I heard it, in surround sound with everyone singing unscripted and in harmony, I was deeply moved. I opened my mouth to sing along but couldn't form any distinguishable words. They came out choppy, faint whispers. I was choking up, eager to join the chorus but emotionally hamstrung by the task. After ten years of avoiding churches, I hadn't expected to find myself here, much less to be undone by a simple hymn: "Let There Be Peace on Earth."

I wouldn't have been there at all if my friend Susie hadn't invited me to her church in St. Paul, Minnesota. My reflexive response was no. Church wasn't my thing. After I left the Episcopal Church in college, I hadn't felt any desire to return to an institution. Susie explained matter-of-factly that it wasn't like Catholic, Lutheran, Episcopal, Methodist or Baptist churches. It was Unity Church—relaxed, friendly, open-minded, and not even very churchy.

To which I replied, "Okay, then why not?"

Walking in that first Sunday, I found myself caught off guard. No organ music, no hymnal-clutching parishioners in their Sunday best. Just people in everyday clothes greeting each other with genuine warmth. Unity is nondenomina-tional. Services aren't steeped in centuries-old ritual. Language is direct.

Worship leaders stepped close to the congregation, break-ing the barrier of separation. Sermons were about everyday matters without reference to larger-than-life Bible moments. It really worked for me. Enough to return—not every Sunday, but many.

That song, though. It always undid me. By the fourth line, I'd crack open, tears streaming, snot running, a lump in my throat making it impossible to join in. It was inexplicable; I knew the song was coming and tried to suck it up each week as the pianist led in. Still, it was a hopeless cause. I preemptively whispered to my neighbors, "I always cry when we sing 'Let There Be Peace On Earth.'" No one minded.

Unity offered space for my own experience to blossom— the small, private ways I felt the presence of something beyond human. With no one expecting anything of me, no external pressure to embrace specific beliefs, I could let my sense of the divine gestate. By this point, the question of god's existence had been answered to my satisfaction. Unity was a spiritual sandbox—a place where I could keep stretching my senses and my awareness, where I could try to press further into what was true about the divine. For a couple of hours each week, I was coaxed into a different state of being.

I wasn't looking to take up a new identity as part of this or any other church. I was a visitor. And yet, I belonged, because everyone truly was welcomed. As the Sundays accumulated, the faces grew familiar. Friendly exchanges about baseball games and sick friends became conversational threads that carried over week to week. I discovered a new kind of connection with people, one that didn't ask anything of either of us, yet naturally invited a desire to offer caring support.

But belonging stirred up its own questions. As a year ticked by, I found myself mulling them over during weekend bike rides around the lakes in Minneapolis: Is this my church? Should I become a member? The implications made me uneasy. I was squeamish about promising to show up every Sunday. While I liked everyone, and felt strong affinity toward a few, joining would yoke me to nice Midwestern folks I barely knew. What did we really have in common? Was my notion of the divine anything like theirs?

I also inferred that a congregant's involvement stretched beyond the walls of the building. Would my weekdays take on new obligations? I liked supporting people I knew and loved, but I hadn't inherited the Good Samaritan gene. Being obligated to help was different from choosing to.

After weeks of this inner push-pull, I met with the minister. She listened as I explained my journey from Episcopal doubt to knowing the divine existed, even if I still stumbled over the word "god." None of this fazed her. But as our conversation unfolded, I sensed her seeing me less as a seeker and more as a potential recruit for church growth. The clarity I'd been missing finally arrived: joining wasn't for me.

I still attended for a while, but something had shifted. My first visit had been pure experience—an expanse of uplifting joy. Now, I felt like church bait, part of someone else's agenda. The Sunday services remained uplifting, that song still made me well up, but I couldn't remain just a visitor passing through.

My departure wasn't an end but a clarification. I was seeking something that couldn't be found within institutional walls, however welcoming they might be.

I surmised that the whole Unity experience signified progress. Just two years earlier, I'd secluded myself at home every night after work trying to think my way out of a post-breakup funk. I'd concluded neither reason nor intuition was functioning well, and hoped that digesting copious texts from theosophical authors—with their blend of Eastern and Western mystical traditions and their intellectual exploration of consciousness and divine wisdom—would right the mental ship. I silently conversed with them while avoiding live conversations with living humans who might want to convince me of their beliefs. I still devoured books in Minneapolis. But the days of holing up were over; I could engage with others' words and wisdom, live and in person, without losing my way.

I also knew that what I was hungry for couldn't be bought in a bookstore or passed down from one person to another. It was intimate, personal, relational, between me and something bigger than me.

In the podcast *Turning to the Mystics*, James Finley tells of his time at a Trappist monastery, where Thomas Merton would ask him, "How's it going with respect to your surrender to the mystery that accessed your heart and brought you to this place that it might transform you into itself?" It probes deeply, and I love the qualities behind that question: agency, choice, direct connection. Inch by inch, I was making my way in relationship to the divine, even though I wasn't anywhere close to surrendering.

I would learn much later that surrender is an incredibly active verb, nothing like its passive implications. I experience surrender as a choice to be taken into something greater than me, despite parts of me kicking and screaming in resistance. Cultivating that will—listening to its appetites, learning to harness and direct it—became a decades-long undertaking, a linchpin of my spiritual journey. I didn't start out as the surrendering type. What began as a flaccid muscle took a lot of exercise before it turned into a spiritual muscle that understood the how, and why, of surrender.

I would also later confirm that I was never hardwired to be a congregant. For me, spiritual community couldn't be fixed in a classical sense. Its form constantly evolved. But there was a clear centerpiece: individuals who possessed keen discernment and who shared my fire for the divine. These were the people I most trusted as I navigated life with my pocketful of burning questions. Many were friends, some were teachers, and for the better part of my life, our interactions took place outside the walls of churches, temples and synagogues.

Only in later years, and quite by accident, did I realize I'd come to rely on a small spiritual community where I found a different kind of harmony. Not a community of faith but of spiritual seekers who were dedicated to practical skill-building in techniques of consciousness. We all embraced a mode that

happened to match my innate proclivity for DIY and JIT—
do-it-yourself and just-in-time.

CHOOSING

ascend

Less than a year after my heart was shattered by barrel-chested, dark-haired Jay in New York, I met another Jay in Orlando, at Disney World. He was blond, tan, a jeans model in college. I'd all but sealed myself off from romance—fraught with peril—and was very happily involved in mergers at work, exercise in the evenings and making friends my age within Procter & Gamble's latest crop of leaders. I was convinced that was all I needed. New Jay, handsome and playful, was my boss's trusted friend who somehow kept finding reasons to talk to me at the conference we attended.

On the second night of entertainment, as the DJ started spinning, Jay charmed me onto the dance floor. He leaned in to ask when my birthday was. I told him, and he said his was the day before mine. I didn't believe it—too much of a coincidence. I needed proof. He teased me as we wrestled; I reached for the wallet in his rear pocket, and he blocked my moves. Finally, I extracted it. Sure enough. Destiny.

Over the next two and a half years, Jay opened my world beyond the career bubble I'd built. A Minnesota boy through and through, he lived in Des Moines but returned often to his tight circle of high school friends. They'd cruise the lakes every summer with motorboats and water skis. I was astonished when he skied barefoot; I'd never seen anything like it. We navigated the distance between us with weekend visits and long phone calls. He showed me the lakes of Minnesota and the State Fair of Iowa and the art of waxing a car. I couldn't help falling in love with him.

For an early-September vacation in Colorado, we packed his Audi with an impressive array of glamping gear. School was back in session and vacation crowds had thinned. Seeing the Rockies in person was much like my introduction to the skyscrapers of New York—jaw-dropping awe at their majestic upshoot toward the sky. It was my highest elevation yet, and my first immersion in the thick golden aspen groves. For almost a week, a quiet campground near the Maroon Bells was our cozy home.

It was my first car-camping adventure—my first camping adventure of any kind, really. I loved it: snuggling in the tent, waking to crisp Alpine air, dining at our picnic table. Jay knew all the tricks to make camping comfortable, and had outfitted us with just-right provisions. Throughout our getaway, I marveled at him, us, and the beauty that enveloped our little slice of heaven.

We hiked every day. I kept up with him on the ascents, but his athleticism and high energy made it easy for him to skip downhill carried by his weight. He'd pause a few feet ahead until I caught up, and then we'd repeat the cycle. It was during one of these warm, sunny hikes that we hit a hitch.

The conversation had turned to god. He was raised Catholic and, despite years without regular church attendance, insisted on the few Catholic beliefs drummed into him as a boy. Paramount was the mediating presence of Jesus. "It's the Father, Son, and Holy Spirit," Jay said. "You can't have a relationship with the Father except through the Son."

"I'm not disputing that all three might exist," I said. "I'm not making the case against any of them. But what's the reason you have to go through the Son to get to the Father?"

"Because it's written in the Bible."

"Do you read the Bible?"

"I have a Bible."

"Do you read it?"

"I haven't in a while. But that's what it says."

"Do you even go to church?"

"I go at Christmas with my family."

"Is that the only time?"

"Yeah." At least he didn't lie.

"Well, I know what I know. And I know what I saw and felt. And I didn't have to go through Jesus. It was a direct experience of god."

"How do you know?"

"I was there. I felt it."

"It can't have happened if you didn't go through Jesus."

I noticed that I was beginning to smolder. Are we really having this conversation? Is he serious?

None of it made sense to me, especially since it seemed on this matter he traded in hearsay. The only way I knew the divine was through direct experience. All the Sunday School classes and sermons and services beginning in childhood and lasting into my twenties hadn't put me in touch with god. The closest I'd come was as a young girl sitting in the pews at my mother's Episcopal church during weddings. I'd choke up without understanding why. My throat would throb, tears would stream down my cheeks, and my heart would swell in my chest. It hurt and was also strangely comforting. I was always relieved when it faded because it felt embarrassingly vulnerable.

"Sorry," I said, "but you can't talk me out of my experience. No matter what you think the Bible says, or even what it does say. That's a bunch of words written centuries ago. They don't know my life. They don't know what happened and how it felt."

It was an incredibly liberating conversation. Not because we agreed—we were violently opposed—but because I stood my ground. I backed myself up instead of deferring to the man I loved, a fatal flaw in my last relationship. This time, there was no impulse to cave.

When we got back to civilization, we tried to find middle ground.

"Let's read the same book about religion," I suggested. "Something that breaks down Catholicism into everyday practical terms. Then we can compare notes."

Someone he knew recommended a Marcus Borg book. I bought the hardcover and read it front to back, marking up passages that seemed to extend permission not to be limited by literal interpretation of the Bible. Ah, I thought, this could work. Borg, a liberal theologist, seems to have space for personal interpretation and reflection. Surely it will open Jay's mind.

Not so fast.

One of us didn't get around to reading the book. Whether it was a result of laziness or a dislike of reading or a reaction to a nonconservative author, I don't know. It would have taken both of us sincerely grappling with the subject matter to have any hope of reaching a new plateau of understanding.

When Jay and I ended things, it was at my suggestion. All the back and forth about god, Christ, and Jay's doctrine of the rules of engagement with the Holy Trinity wore me out. He still wasn't attending church outside of big holidays but remained adamant. As was I. How could anyone negotiate away the fact of a direct connection to the divine? We could move forward together only if one of us was willing to live a lie. When that sad truth dawned on me, I shared my conclusion with him. He couldn't disagree.

We could have prolonged the relationship, focusing on our love and common interests instead of this one chasm. After all, we technically shared the zone of Christianity. But once the clearest-eyed perspectives we could muster were out in the open, creating a roadblock that wouldn't budge, why try to build a life together?

So, we let love die.

I was alone in my apartment sitting on the couch after our final conversation. I stared into space feeling empty and grasping for the bearings that our relationship had afforded me. My chest physically hurt. How could someone I love so much be taken from me? Taken not by another lover or by illness, but by something we both deemed insurmountable.

At first, I felt sorry for myself. It was a pity party. I was convinced by my complaint that it shouldn't be this way. I told myself I'd been wronged. Cheated. Something I wanted had been stolen from me.

Distraught, I started to cry. Then I sobbed, heaving on the in-breath. The whole situation seemed so unfair to my damsel in distress.

As dramatic as it felt, it was a surface layer of emotion. Protective behavior, really. By casting myself as a casualty of love, I could avoid the deeper hurt. I could be mad at something, point a finger, blame, make the story about an issue "out there." Anything but the simple, crushing pain in my heart that had nowhere to go.

Through some kind of grace, within about fifteen minutes I opened—ceasing to brace against the flurry of thoughts and sensations racing through me. I stopped trying to escape, dodge, and deflect the pain. I stopped arguing reality. The truth was, we weren't a fit. Love wouldn't change it. And it sucked.

When I finally reached my low, the place where I knew in my bones the argument was over and I had nothing left to lose, I said to myself, "Okay, let's feel this. Let's go in."

Then I broke down and sobbed like a child.

I wailed so hard I had to cover my mouth with a pillow to keep from freaking out the neighbors. I didn't want them to hear me and worry, and I surely didn't want a thoughtful knock at my door. In that moment, I didn't want sympathy or rescue. I wanted to see what would happen if I plunged myself directly into the center of the pain. For god's sake, don't interrupt me now that I'm finally beyond resistance.

It went on for a while. The tears came from such a deep place, a place so wordless, that my mind was blank. All that existed was raw feeling. I allowed my body to express it through sobs followed by air gulps and then more sobs.

Then, a pop. The space changed.

A light.

Brightness.

Warmth.

Enveloping me.

Space of pure serenity.

Wholeness and fullness and completeness.

Love. Massive love. Pouring in.

Love that surpasses all understanding.

That's what they mean.

This, this, this.

Wherever it came from, it was here now.

Oh.

Releasing into its fold.

Held. Comforted. Shown.

Heart, blasted open.

Richer than a love affair.

Real.

No need to trust. Simple. Is.

Always.

And there I was. Sitting in silence. Taken in. Taken through. On the other side of the protective wall of my heart. It had opened to something so glorious I was speechless. My face turned up toward the invisible presence that shrouded me in nonphysical light. I was unarmed. Pliable. Capable of receiving whatever gifts from non-physical worlds that were being spilled into me. Some part of me had known how to put out the call. Some part of me knew how to receive what was being offered.

Pain never felt or looked the same after that.

It's not a bogeyman out to make me miserable. I don't have to dodge it in order to enjoy a good life. Quite the opposite. If pain's there, I'm better off acknowledging and feeling it. Though the act of opening seems to follow a different path each time I choose to do it.

moan

Tom Brady, according to interviews and lore, treats his body like a temple. I don't go that far, but I have a version. Purified water is nonnegotiable, organic produce fills my grocery cart, and my protein sources often don't include red meat. Exercise is vital—to build stamina and give me an outlet when I'm emotionally charged.

When I was stressed out by one of my corporate jobs, I integrated massage into my regime. Again, not daily like Brady. I went every other week. Until my masseuse tipped me off.

"If you did yoga, you wouldn't need massage."

I was lying face down on Albert's table as he kneaded out my back. He was a tall, hulking figure with thick dark hair and long, muscular fingers. He saw clients in his home. His other income stream was as a yoga instructor at a swanky athletic club in Portland.

I didn't care for the tip and barely mumbled "Hmmm." I liked the passive feeling of being cared for, of someone else taking responsibility for how I felt for three hours a month.

Yoga sounded like work. Albert let the idea go. Until the next visit, and then the next. Given his dual occupation, he had the cred to make such an assertion. At the very least, it was worth considering.

At the time, I ran communications for a national insurance company. Tony, my peer in investor relations, proposed that my team oversee production of the annual report. I took it as a vote of confidence and agreed, despite never having done one. After all, if the accountability belonged to my department, we'd figure it out.

Early in the project Tony began showing signs of doubt, questioning almost every step and every deliverable. Advancing the project was painstaking, not because of the work itself, but because of our incompatible styles. My team was creative, Tony was analytical. We were fluid, he was methodical. While the learning curve was predictable, managing Tony's ever-growing concern was not. If at any moment the ship wasn't battened down—or didn't appear to be battened down—his temples tensed and his voice tightened. He viewed the report, rightly so, as a tool for strong positioning among investors and analysts. He raised the idea, midstream, of having an outside firm take over. It took a toll on the team lead, and eventually on me. I spent more time reassuring him we could get the job done than actually doing it.

Late nights piled up as we toiled through concepting, drafting, editing, reviewing and revising the report. The final product left a positive impression with Wall Street analysts who mattered. My team, however, had residual bruises. Recovery didn't come from my usual outlets—cycling, weightlifting, gardening. It came, unexpectedly, in an aerobics room that doubled as a yoga studio, three blocks from the office.

One Tuesday evening at 6:40 p.m., I walked away from the project to take my first yoga class. In loose sweats, I claimed the far corner of the dimly lit studio, as far from the instructor as possible. He was a slight man of few words; his style was to show, not tell. We started with breath, lying on our backs, arms to our sides, observing our chests as they rose and fell. After about ten minutes, he demonstrated how to elongate our bodies on the mat by drawing our head, neck, and shoulders in one direction, hips in the other. I kept waiting for him to take us into the poses plastered across magazine covers: down dog, warrior II, standing prayer. He never went there. The whole evening was spent in some form of recline or floor stretch.

As I followed his lead, the jabber in my mind grew quieter. The weight of my body really did sink into the floor. Halfway through the session, I moaned aloud. The sound escaped before I could catch it. I glanced around, embarrassed, but it seemed no one had noticed. By the end of class, my meridians had been wrung out like a soaking-wet towel. Finally, full relaxation and a mind at complete rest without slumbering.

The next week, I went back. And the next. The instructor never discussed technique or meditation. He just kept moving us into twists, folds, and stretches that released whatever we were carrying. And I kept moaning as inconspicuously as possible. I'd always viewed yoga as too passive, too slow for my driven nature. Were these quiet evenings allowing me to connect with a part of myself that ambition hid from view?

A few months later, I tried a weekend class at a gym closer to home. Jen, a fit woman in her thirties with short dark hair, spoke with clarity and precision and floated through the room offering barely there adjustments when she spotted potential injury. Her class became my Saturday ritual. Word was, she was the best. We watched her belly grow as she taught through her pregnancy nearly to term. She eventually went on maternity leave, and the sub didn't hold a candle to her. That's when I realized I'd been learning from a master.

Once again, it was direct experience, not someone's word for it, that won me over. The most charming Indian yogi in the world couldn't have convinced me that yoga would change my life. That I'd come to lust after altered states of body and mind.

Three years after Albert first suggested I do yoga, I canceled my standing massage appointments and migrated to four- to six-week intervals. I might never get better at crow pose—I'm comically imbalanced—but I can rock a modified forearm stand against the wall. Nowadays I return to yoga at least twice a week to prevent what I call energetic constipation. Otherwise, I end up with fitful sleep, weaker concentration, mild uneasiness, and growing malaise.

One evening, having missed a few days of yoga, I was charged up and needed to decompress. The refrigerator and the TV were awfully tempting, but I knew neither would give me the relief I craved. So, I rolled out my mat and got down on all fours to arch, bend and follow a sequence I enjoy. When I reached warrior II, my vagus nerve released. The din of tension was replaced by a silent internal hum. I let out a few long moans. As loud as I wanted.

living the dream

I sat up on the side of my bed, my eyes fixed on the white floorboard, where two invisible paths stretched out before me. One screamed security—the retirement package growing handsomely each year, the known routine, a life insured against upheaval. The other pulsed with an aliveness that couldn't be denied. After months of dreams filled with tumbling fragments, the choice to be made was finally clear.

The dream had built itself slowly, like a jigsaw puzzle refusing to reveal its full image. Night after night, small sections would click into place, each new piece casting light on the greater picture emerging. Some areas began to stand out with startling clarity, while others remained shrouded. The abstract gradually became concrete, building toward something I could feel but not yet fully grasp.

For months, though, one piece remained stubbornly elusive. Each morning, I'd reach back into that liminal space between sleep and waking, trying to snatch it up, but the last click that would complete the picture stayed just beyond my grasp.

Until this morning, when it followed me effortlessly from slumber into consciousness.

There it all was. Splayed out before me to ponder. Two paths. With them came a straightforward choice—to go one direction or the other.

Movement to the left meant little change; staying in the job. Going to the right meant major change; leaving for destinations unknown, and the potential for aliveness without guarantees.

On the one hand, it was that simple. That pure. No judgment of any kind. No hint about what would be best for me. On the other hand, it was brimming with information far beyond mental understanding—not merely about the choice, but also about the qualities and experiences I could expect.

If I chose the leftward direction, I'd have employment and all the stability, financial and emotional, that came with it. I couldn't tell how long into the future I'd stay at the company, but it felt like years if not decades; the trajectory dissolved into a misty distance. The overall tone was staid and safe. Which made sense. The excitement of my first few years employed there was long gone; the rush of building a high-performing communications team and running a national branding campaign was over.

The right reeked of daring adventure. While there was no telling what would come, it felt vibrant and zesty. The implicit and explicit assurances that come with a fixed day job wouldn't be there, but neither would the humdrum. I'd be turning toward the unknown. An open road with novelty but no preview of coming attractions.

The dream didn't include a warning light. There was no nudge to subtly guide me in one direction or the other. Neither choice was better than the other. The neutrality of how the options were displayed was almost surreal. Whatever I wanted for my life was perfectly fine. One hundred percent.

It was a true choice. That, itself, was marked.

I sensed that going to the right would require tapping into parts of myself that had gone dormant or had never been ignited in the first place. It would be a decidedly nonpassive way of life. There would be no coasting. That's what I'd sacrifice if I left the job.

The word selection above is an approximation. The truth is, I knew all of this in an instant, received the flash of illumination in less than a second. There was an insistence that my decision simply and only be based on what I wanted deep inside, given what I understood to be possible with either direction.

Well, I thought, that's easy.

The human animal in me cherishes comfort and order. If that were the only criteria, I'd obviously turn left.

My human spirit didn't want that. Not. At. All. The promise of comfort paled in comparison to the prospect of aliveness.

The right was so compelling that it almost wasn't a choice. I had to go.

I was still in my pajamas sitting up in my bed. I understood the dream. I understood the choice. The decision was immediate. Zero mental processing, worry, drama or analysis. In the absence of any consternation whatsoever, it was clear as day.

The only matter left to consider was how long to wait before giving notice at work. But that was oddly clear, too: twenty-one days.

I'd wait until then to take it up with my boss. Assuming all that had finally become clear didn't dissipate—if it didn't look like a silly fantasy by that time—I'd go.

I'm fortunate to have had fantastic bosses throughout my career. Every supervisor valued what I did and how I did it. They gave me as much rope to run with as I wanted. Mike, the executive I worked for at the time, was no exception.

Three weeks after I made my decision, I told him I needed to resign. I offered more details than an employee would typically disclose. Mike and I were open with each other about our respective spiritual quests. We were both seekers. By day he was a corporate attorney; on vacation he studied with spiritual teachers and on weekends he painted as a serious artist. I trusted him.

My announcement took him by surprise. He asked me to reconsider. Together we pondered whether we could create a new role at the company that would entice me to stay. I had a strong suspicion it was a fool's errand, though I also felt it would be worthwhile if covering all the possible bases meant I'd never look back and regret leaving. I was, after all, walking away from a future that many would covet.

My official notice period was four weeks—more than enough time to position my team well for the transition. Mike and all my colleagues were magnanimous, throwing multiple going-away parties. My heart swelled, as I genuinely liked my colleagues across all the departments and divisions. With each goodbye, I felt a tiny emotional tug, a flash of awareness that we'd no longer be part of each other's lives, solving problems together and bringing the company's vision to life. I felt ridiculous for tearing up so often when simultaneously I was tickled to be moving on.

As my last day, a Friday, approached, I contemplated the open road ahead. Nothing fixed. Nothing known about what was to come. A blank canvas. I didn't want to feel lost and eerily alone with nowhere to go on that Monday. I didn't want to feel bored when my channel for feeling valuable and productive was no longer there.

I did a little research in advance to find a yoga class. It ran at 8:00 a.m. every weekday. It was nearby, so I could cycle there. This would be my first baby step into a new routine. A little something to ground me and introduce a new, simple focus.

This first, tiny step served its purpose beautifully. Shadow yoga was new to me, but learner mode comes naturally. The method wasn't easy. My knees weren't entirely up to the challenge. More accurately, my knees felt the effects of movement that depended on thigh and buttocks strength. I didn't have it to start. Oh, well. That's the point. Focus on something new that I could develop with practice.

So far, so good.

This is the typical point in the story where one would expect the protagonist to encounter an obstacle. She's made a big decision. Change is afoot. She can't see around the corner. BAM! Surprise! A big bad challenge makes things hard. Then, she'll overcome it and, in the process, learn something that changes her worldview.

Naw. That's not this story.

What happened next was utterly magical: three days when everything, everywhere, fell effortlessly into its perfect place. I suppose it's what people mean when they talk about flow. It was all-encompassing. Not like losing myself in a project that took on a life of its own. More like connecting with a divine hand offering gentle nudges to say, "Turn left here . . . Look up now . . . Talk to this person . . . Go into that store you never noticed."

It was as though I'd hopped on an invisible conveyor belt that moved me with great precision through space, time and experiences of pure delight. I can't recall exact details, just that every move was deliberate. My part was simple: to go along for the ride. Moment after moment was teeming with life as it should and could be. I couldn't have masterminded anything so full and profound and simple and dialed in to a cosmos far bigger than me. I went to bed at night feeling so grateful for the day. And aware that surely this couldn't last.

For seventy-two hours, I was privy to a font of grace. It gave me a new appreciation for creation itself. The new-age books I'd read in my twenties and thirties said people can tap into it at will, but that's not how this felt. Grace is not a commodity. It cannot be bartered.

Looking back, it wasn't the choice that invited the magic. It was the still, quiet place in me from which the choice was made. The Quakers have a special way of describing what I think was happening. They call it "the leading of the spirit." I was surely being led. And I said yes, all in.

Part II
Going In

There is a voice that doesn't use words.

Listen.

widely attributed to Rumi

MEDITATING

om

In the mid-1980s, before leaving New York City, I received the rarest of treats. Loni, the friend who'd introduced me to channeling, invited me to an evening with Gurumayi. To be exact, it was with Gurumayi's students. They gathered regularly to meditate, and I was one of their guests for an evening of chanting.

With eyes closed, everyone repeated the mantra: Om Namah Shivaya. It wasn't merely spoken; it had a melody that rose and fell, moving through a harmony that left me sinking deeper with each repetition. Everyone knew it by heart. After listening to a few rounds, I knew the progression well enough to join the chorus. In twenty minutes, I was thoroughly intoxicated. Transported to a dimension I didn't know existed. No mental ramblings. Just a vast space, broad and open, where I felt overwhelming calm and stillness. My voice didn't create the chant—it rode on it.

The vast openness I landed in was too beautiful to abandon. I didn't want my altered state of consciousness to end. Ever. As Gurumayi's students completed the last round, it was almost painful to open my eyes and return to this world.

Nothing in the next two decades rose to that rarefied bliss. I tried a few techniques at home: Listening to a recording of Gurumayi leading the chant and following instructions on the breath. Sitting when I felt an impulse to do so, never regularly. By and large, though, these solo attempts proved fruitless. My inner voice dominated. That stillness was nowhere to be found.

I filed meditation away as something other people did. People with more motivation and more talent in mind silencing than I had. I wasn't missing out on an especially good thing, and I liked the way life was unfolding. I was living in Portland and had recently left my corporate job. No longer constricted by an office, I could enjoy distance cycling on weekdays and weekends alike. It became a true joy—riding with a local club and experiencing personal connections that had little to do with personalities. A slow and steady march to learn Spanish prompted a few trips to Spain, each one its own unique experience of different towns, cities and regions. I began independent consulting. It wasn't just a livelihood; it satisfied a desire to create good things with good people.

When my best friend, Paulina, moved to Portland, I was delighted to have her take over my second bedroom. She had started meditating. She hadn't really wanted to—and didn't like it very much—but it was a prerequisite for courses on space clearing, and she was passionate about becoming a clearer. For fifteen to twenty minutes after she woke up, she kept her bedroom door closed and meditated. We never talked about what it was like, only about her displeasure at having to do it.

A few months later, she shared a realization. "I don't love sitting, but I love the result."

It confirmed the changes I was noticing in her. Limiting beliefs that used to bind her no longer held sway. She was turning into the person she'd always wanted to be, moving toward things that held intrigue and splendor rather than holding back. Since we lived under the same roof, I was a steady witness to this gradual shift in attitude. Her expansion kept gaining momentum and there was no backsliding. The changes became obvious to anyone close to her.

Seeing what was happening for Paulina sparked something in me. It stirred a desire I didn't know I had, with more force than the pull in me to cycle, travel and work. I wanted what she had. I wanted my version of what I saw underway from her simple, twenty-minute investment every morning.

Maybe it's not pie in the sky to want a certain kind of change—even if it can't be fully articulated—and expect it can happen. There was only one way to find out. In Paulina, I witnessed proof enough of the possibility.

She told me to get Samuel Sagan's *Awakening the Third Eye* because it detailed how to do the meditation she was practicing. I tracked down a used copy at Powell's Books in downtown Portland. Sure enough, it had a step-by-step guide. I read the first four chapters, memorized the steps and then gave it a go.

Unlike other methods of meditation, this one didn't focus on breath or mantras. Instead, it drew attention to distinct qualities of vibration, light and sound. They were easy to notice within a few minutes of sitting with eyes closed and shifting awareness to the energetic third eye—between and slightly above the eyebrows. Simple as they sounded, those qualities gave my consciousness a resting place, a figurative cushioned pad on which to let go. To my amazement, the effect was striking. My mind quieted, my nerves relaxed and I noticed a kind of inner peace I never felt in waking life. The closest I'd come to it before was in deep, restorative sleep.

Since my goal was to see if a meditation practice could change my life in good ways, I had to start by turning those fifteen minutes into a habit. I decided I would go for forty consecutive days. I'd heard that this was how long it took to form a permanent habit. I kept my promise to myself, even when I traveled cross-country to visit my parents for a week. In my home, I had a dedicated corner for meditation in my bedroom. In their home, I had to rig a new setup in their spare room using throw pillows from living room furniture.

When I reached forty days, what I wanted next was clear: keep it up. Consistency would further ingrain the habit. As the weeks passed, I enjoyed deeper levels of well-being as a reward for my fifteen minutes of focus on the qualities that sprung from third-eye awareness.

Then, I started to notice something curious. Any day I didn't meditate turned funky, fast. That quarter of an hour produced so much synchronicity that I felt deprived on the rare days I skipped. When I bailed on my morning sit, thinking I could better use those fifteen minutes elsewhere, the whole day seemed to unravel. My body had learned what my mind was still figuring out: this practice wasn't optional anymore.

I could have settled nicely into this serene morning ritual with its reliable payoff and called it good. It worked, and I liked doing it much more than Paulina seemed to. Each morning, my nervous system was at ease and my brain was at rest as I migrated from a state of doing to a state of being—without trying. But calling it good wasn't good enough for me. Once I'd tasted this new orientation, I was intrigued by what might be around the corner.

The effect spread to my life off the mat, so when I opened my eyes, I was no longer up against familiar obstacles; ephemeral things somehow fell into their rightful places. There were tasks to do, but the way I approached them was different. It was as if I plugged into something above this world, and in doing so, two subtle but noteworthy things happened on an increasingly consistent basis.

Synchronicity seemed to seek me out. With less exertion, I was connecting with new people, and invitations appeared out of nowhere. Plans came together without effort. My orientation was rearranging, too. I was animated in a fresh way, attuned to something bigger than me that participated in the unfolding of each moment of the day. I didn't hear voices. No, it was more like an infusion into the marrow of my bones, creating a subtle, all-over sensation that couldn't be traced or defined. How it worked was mysterious. I was connected to a field of energy outside myself. Me, plus more.

In a few short months, daily life felt different. The shift was subtle. Quiet. I was gently transposed. No control or drive on my part. Just a willingness to show up every day, and sufficient awareness to notice that it brought good changes.

This wasn't so different from the experience I'd had twenty years earlier while chanting with Gurumayi's devotees. Something about that singular evening had stayed with me all these years, whispering of possibilities beyond my everyday experience. Now, from this surprising plateau, I sensed a door cracking open to those larger spaces. The practice had changed me more in a few months than I could have imagined. I had to know what lay on the other side.

the Catskills

My first meditation retreat was in upstate New York, twenty years after I left New York City. It was nearly as far as one could go from Oregon, where I lived, and remain stateside. I'd signed up for the introductory course, in July. My brother and his girlfriend picked me up at JFK airport on their way to Woodstock and dropped me off in the Catskills. We hugged goodbye, and I grew flush, some part of me knowing a new threshold was around the corner.

The ten-day event was well-paced, running from 8:30 a.m. to 9:30 p.m. every day; there were group meditations, paired practices, talks and vegetarian meals. The highlight of every student's afternoon was the forty-five-minute night practice—like a nap on steroids.

We also learned IST (Inner Space Techniques), a set of techniques to surface and release old emotional wounds. During this partner exercise, I was invited to explore in ways that took some getting used to. Instead of conjuring emotions and narratives of past experiences, I was encouraged to direct my attention toward qualities that were more tactile— to notice sensations such as hot or cold, soft or hard, moving or still, etc. When my mind reverted to interpretation, my IST partner gently steered me back. Distraught and helpless when I was in utero? Go into the feeling rather than try to understand. Angry from a past life of unjust imprisonment? Stay with the experience, not the story. Talk less, feel more.

Most sessions didn't conclude with epiphanies. They did, however, expose my proclivity to rationalize—to manage, rather than open, as a form of self-protection. With time, things big and small that had plagued me began to resolve, but not by my picking them apart with analysis. IST invited a nonverbal, nonmental side of me to get involved, alongside a presence that's not atypical in churches, synagogues and mosques. A numinous presence that could seep into the deepest pores of my being and rearrange things in ways that I couldn't do on my own. Was it the same exact presence I experienced in other mystical moments of my life? Maybe. But for me, divine presence tends to feel more composite than individual, and I've come to see that the distinction doesn't usually matter.

Here was the depth I'd expected to find when I decided to take my meditation practice to the next level. I liked it so much, I stayed for two more courses and a total of three weeks

I got in the habit of walking the gentle two-mile loop on the property in the morning before we all gathered. The next workshop, about vortices, was co-led by two men: a computer programmer and a veterinarian. To help us connect with vortices, they played recordings with deep sounds that made me feel as though I were spinning backward into space. They frequently referenced "superior stillness," a new term to me. My initial inference was that it meant moving as little as possible; be like a stone, freeze in place. They themselves were the personification of stillness. Both could plop onto their mats, cross their legs, close their eyes, and in no time flat, leave ordinary mental consciousness behind. I was impressed.

I did my best. I didn't wiggle my body every few minutes to get comfortable. I didn't reflexively scratch. I didn't sneeze or cough. But did I achieve true superior stillness in that one week? No way. It was an advanced state, but having gotten a taste, I knew I'd recognize it as I inched closer.

The extended stay at the center gave me plenty to work with when I returned to Oregon. My meditations effortlessly stretched to twenty or thirty minutes, sometimes as long as forty. And I took advantage of the school's correspondence courses, absorbing knowledge and practices at my own pace from the comfort of home.

A year later at the same center, I discovered what superior stillness can do. The course was almost full, and we were packed tightly in a meeting room. The instructor guided us through a practice that lasted about forty-five minutes, right up to the lunch hour. As he slowly brought everyone out of the exercise, I lingered in the ethers and basked in the experience. It was full-on. Bliss. Wonder. Awe. Delight. I didn't want to come back. As everyone rose to leave for their meal, I remained oblivious.

A student approached me from behind. She said my name. I was so far away, it sounded dreamlike. She said it again. That did it. The meditation was over, the moment gone.

The descent back to earth began. It was still several moments before I could open my mouth to reply. When she knew she had my attention, she spoke again.

"I want to talk about that email you sent," she said.

Holy shit. She pulled me back for that? A minor upset? It turned out to be next to nothing, and she could have said something a week earlier. She could have pulled me aside during a meal. But no. She released a fluctuation—through an audible sound wave and energetic pinprick—when we were the last two people in the temple. It was a stunning killjoy. I tumbled down, down, back to earth from this high state of consciousness and refined silence. Ah, I thought. This must be what people in the meditation school mean when they talk about crashing the space.

Some meditations propel my consciousness into such an altered state that it takes a while to come back to awareness of my surroundings afterward. It's a bit like when my alarm rings in the morning and I can't put together what the sound is and where it's coming from. My senses are entirely offline; my body is there, but I'm not in it. Gradually, there's a reentry. Sound, light, smell and touch turn on. When I've been in really deep, it takes an act of will to reanimate any part of my body. The first movements feel forced and borderline violent. That's a sign of superior stillness.

For me, that level of stillness and silence is not the end goal. It's a portal that opens doors into much bigger spaces.

A necessary step. Once I experienced it, it was only natural to want more. Then I was ready to learn how to establish a pathway to return to stillness, again and again.

As I was gathering new skills and references, I jumped at the chance to be part of a weekly study group with students from the US and Canada. Six of us self-organized to meet online weekly. I also made annual treks to the retreat center in New York for in-person courses. When the school's headquarters moved to Northern California, I could drive to the new retreat center in eight hours, taking in majestic forests of Nordic pine and high volcanic desert along the way. Now, I aim to spend two or three weeks a year there. It's good for my soul.

Whether I'm in the temple at the meditation center or in the solitude of my home, receptivity is a natural byproduct when I settle down, quiet down and open. My guard drops. My driving nature moves to the back seat so something bigger can take over.

It's a form of surrender—physically, mentally, emotionally.

From this position, I can be guided. I can be shown things that otherwise would be imperceptible. Just as importantly, I can listen. As I listen, I can discern:

This is my own schtick.

But now, this is something else entirely; I don't have a reference for it. That's okay. In fact, it's better than okay.

The loss of references comes with entering newer

dimensions I was unaware of. Without my mind running its endless loop, I'm free to explore.

This lifestyle choice—meditating each morning and practicing regularly with peers—began transforming every corner of my life in unexpected ways. At first, the changes showed up in my body. At the gym, I found myself doubling the weights I could lift, accessing a deeper reservoir of strength. On group bike rides, I rode with new confidence and power, easily holding my place in pace lines that would have dropped me before. But the real surprise came in my work. Clients began commenting that my consulting approach was unlike anything they'd seen before. What I used to call intuition had expanded into something closer to vision, a clarity that let me see straight to the heart of complex situations. I was throwing my whole self—heart, mind, and belly—into everything that mattered to me, and the results were undeniable.

A calm mind, the obvious promise of meditation, was an early and predictable outcome. What emerged over time was breathtaking. I'm both softer and stronger. More open and more focused. Less constrained. Faster to action. Capable in ways never imagined.

Applied with the mindset of a warrior, meditation turned out to be a tool for reinventing myself. It combusts and dissolves, constructs and fortifies, pierces illusion and illuminates truth, a force of change from deep within. Little did I know that securing a habit would lead to vast experiences of this world and worlds beyond—to pushing past physical, intellectual and emotional limits.

mushrooms

On a rare sunny day during spring in London, I walked through a neighborhood with a new friend. Jeff, a Pomona College student with a broad jaw and especially thick brown hair, stopped midsentence to stare at pink blooms on the cherry tree across the street. We'd met during a semester abroad at the London School of Economics.

"Wow, that would be so cool on shrooooooms!" He was mesmerized.

"What would it be like?" I asked.

Rather than roll his eyes at my naiveté, he indulged me by attempting to describe a pleasurable drug trip.

Out of your mind.

Colorful.

Surreal.

Blissful.

You don't want it to end.

I was happy for him, that he had experiences he savored. Drugs had taken him to places of awe, with the exception of one nightmarish episode he later described. All the good outweighed the risk, so he planned to keep it up.

Based on what friends told me over the years about substances they tried, I suspected my drug of choice would be ecstasy or cocaine. Open hearts? Yes, please. Focused, faster thinking? Ditto. A lot of kids at my high school took their fair share of illegal drugs; they smoked them, ate them, popped them—everything short of injecting them. I politely declined when invited. I didn't want to risk getting kicked out, faltering on a varsity team, or messing up my grades. I needed to protect my brain. I needed every bit of concentration I could muster to not fall behind.

I realized much later there was another reason: I probably would have liked mind-altering drugs too much. That hunch was confirmed when I was prescribed Vicodin postsurgery. It was heavenly. Who could argue with how great it felt? When I got a taste of what I'd been missing, I was grateful I'd had enough wits about me as a teenager to pass on it altogether.

Once meditation became an anchor in my life, I understood Jeff's fascination with the cherry tree. Pre-meditation, I lacked any real reference for altered states. I couldn't imagine being suspended in a way that would make me want to keep letting go. Presences in other realms, clearly not of this world, with their own intelligence and purpose for existence, were nowhere on my radar. Only through meditation did glorious levels of consciousness come into sharp relief.

silent med

I meditated daily for over two years and attended five week-long meditation courses before I tried my first silent retreat. It, too, lasted a week. In the dead of winter. Snow blanketed the landscape, which greatly enhanced the sense of quiet in the air.

Given the hype about how hard it is to sit through silent meditation day after day, I was worried it might not go well. But I loved it. Every. Single. Day. And night. My mind grew quieter as days passed with fewer thought fluctuations. It felt like gradually peeling back layers of an onion that I'd only ever experienced at a silly surface level. The deeper I went, the less there was to say and the more space there was inside for consciousness to simply circulate. Consciousness recognizing itself. It was so . . . simple. Yet so profound.

As for being around twenty other meditators, none of whom spoke to or even looked at each other when we passed in the dining hall or on the grounds of the retreat center, it was awkward at first. But before long, it felt liberating. No small talk. No courtesies to extend. We could all just be in our cocoons. I wasn't lonely. I was free to plunge into spaces without anyone interrupting them, without having to explain them, without someone else's story interrupting my own.

The next silent retreat I attended had an even softer quality about it. Nevertheless, it packed the power of a jackhammer and the precision of a scalpel. I got chiseled in the best sense of the word. Things I didn't want to carry anymore were lifted. What were they exactly? That, I can't say. I just felt the tangibility of being unburdened.

So, I'm a big believer in silent meditation retreats.

It's always interesting to me when I hear folks talk about going to a silent meditation retreat stone cold, having never meditated before. If they choose a program that involves sitting hour after hour, listening to their own breathing, with no talk allowed anywhere for seven to ten days, then they're living out the *Thelma & Louise* of meditation. Gunning it out over a cliff. I would have tangled myself in knots of impatience and frustration.

When friends say they're thinking about doing a silent retreat as their first meditation experience, I suggest they think twice. I couldn't have done it. Well, I have discipline and will. I could have toughed it out, as many people do. But it would have been an exercise in endurance, not transcendence. I needed a foundation first. A reliable method I could follow for resting my consciousness so that my mind could slip into a quieter state. I had to build subtle muscles—a scaffolding of experience that strengthened my ability not just to reach silence, but also to sustain it, to hold it for longer and longer stretches of time. Having covered some key bases in advance, I succeeded in minimizing the unpleasant surprises of silent meditation retreats, leaving me to revel in the good ones.

you had to be there

Trying to describe meditation to a person who's never experienced its release is like trying to explain orgasms to someone who's never had sex. It's experiential, and technique matters.

I happened to stumble on a technique that allows me to get the upper hand over the gyrations of my monkey mind. I don't presume it's for everyone, and there are plenty of other techniques—ancient and newer—that deliver results. It simply works well for me.

When I'm asked about meditation by someone interested in trying it out, what I want to know before I offer a suggestion is what they want. What are they trying to achieve? Meditation as a concept sounds pretty good, but there are so many options. It used to be you had to go somewhere to learn. Now smartphone apps are popular. I want more than quieting my mind. Yet for many people that's their goal, and it's no small thing. It seems to me that shopping around can't hurt. I'm not familiar enough with all that's out there to advise which one to try first (though, as mentioned, I can suggest thinking twice before starting with a silent retreat). But I can sniff out the difference between a longing for inner peace and a quest for the divine. Either way, it's an adventure to test different techniques.

A close friend took the introductory weekend class offered through my meditation school. She was intrigued by what started to open for her, and a few months later enrolled in an on-site class in California. According to her, it was like nothing she'd ever done. She was flooded with spiritual connections that felt strangely familiar. I could tell by the way she described her meditation and related practices how plugged in she was to benevolent forces.

However, the structure of our training didn't fit for her in the long run. She found another community of meditators that was a better match for who she is and what she wants and the lifestyle she leads. She's gone the distance and is now an ordained monk.

Another friend, who meditates using a different technique, read a passage I wrote about one of my morning meditations. He quipped that his never go as far as mine seemed to go. He reaches stillness, calm and quiet. But rarely bliss.

"I'll have what she's having" was basically what he was saying, reminiscent of the famous diner scene in *When Harry Met Sally*. He wondered what I did that was different from what he did.

I couldn't say for sure because I don't know enough about the specifics of his practice, and even if I did, it's not the practice I've been in for years. I lack the necessary references to properly answer his question. What I do know is that I don't experience meditation as just me, alone, sitting on a pillow. I have a sense of a living tradition that engages with me in the practice.

It's not unlike the way spiritual traditions come to life through various religions. To call it a force is quite accurate. Real, alive and active. So, part of what happens when I meditate is I come into greater alignment with these forces. It feels . . . wonderful. It's not emotional or particularly sensory because the experience happens beyond the physical dimension. One way to describe it is that my essence commingles with that of angelic presences. That's pretty darn sweet. It doesn't happen on command, only through quieting the mind, involuting, being aware of the qualities of the space as they evolve and opening to be with what's there.

I sometimes wonder if a mindfulness app would have been good for my younger self. It's conceivable that my mind would have fought it tooth and nail. On the other hand, it could have been helpful, a training ground to develop references for what quiet feels like and the navigation of internal landscapes to get there. The thing I can't know without actually taking the apps for a test-drive is what they would plug me into. In other words, the forces behind them. What I know now that I didn't know then is that opening my consciousness involves an interface. I'm not opening to nothing. These spaces of consciousness can be infused with something incredibly tangible, incredibly mysterious, or both.

dive in

y father stood beside me in the waves at Atlantic Beach, North Carolina. The ocean broke around my seven-year-old torso while barely reaching his thighs. Another wall of water topped with white foam rolled toward us. My legs wobbled from the sudden pressure.

"The trick," he said, "is to dive straight into it."

I must have looked at him in disbelief. Dive into that roaring mass of water? But he was already demonstrating, lifting his arms over his head, bending his knees, and lunging directly into the oncoming wave crest. He disappeared beneath the churning foam while I remained, watching the spot where he'd vanished, sure the wave had run him into the sandy bottom, as it had done to me so often. I was relieved when he surfaced on the far side of the waves. He snapped his head to the left to get the hair out of his eyes and then called to me. "It's completely calm under there. It's only scary when you don't go down far enough."

It took several more waves, more patient coaching, and finally his hand holding mine before I tried it. We dove together, and after the initial shock, I felt it—that unexpected pocket of stillness beneath the chaos. He was right. There was hidden calm amidst the roil.

Four decades later, I'd discover the same principle in meditation. Beyond the turbulent surface of my chattering mind lay a profound stillness. It was there, waiting for me. But I had to learn how to traverse the noise.

Once I believed silence could open new doors, I changed things up. I turned down the volume on the home stereo and car radio. I didn't need to get jacked up. I used to play classical music when I worked at the computer and stopped when I realized I could connect with clearer thoughts and bigger ideas, and more quickly, without it. The clutter on my desk created its own version of noise. The stacks of paper, file folders, notebooks and books disappeared into filing cabinets and shelves. With clearness came clarity and, from time to time, hints of originality.

Now, I cherish long stretches of pure silence when I'm deep in thought—responding to clients, writing, learning something new. Ideas can bubble up. When I can't quite unlock a thought form, I pause, attune and listen, and when the flow resumes, I follow it.

There are, however, three exceptions to my unofficial silence treaty: birds, crickets and frogs. I can't get enough of them, unless I'm meditating or sleeping. Then, shroud me in silence, please.

Why silence? So I can hear. Hear myself. Hear the divine. Getting there isn't as simple as turning off the music, though. Some people believe silence is annoying, a trickster, something to be endured. But I've come to understand it's not silence that my mind resists—it's the dual assault of internal and external noise. Internally, left unchecked, my mind unleashes torrents of chatter, a favorite being the obsessive replay of conversations, perfecting what I should have said hours or days too late. Externally, the calculated provocations of the media, designed not just to inform but to inflame me, vie for my attention. In the beginning, trying to turn off the noise does elicit a trick. The noise gets louder. In reality, it's just that an isolated noise seems louder in contrast to whatever silence is taking root in the background.

Am I immune? Not at all. I can succumb to dopamine rushes from quick-fire emails and texts sent from those devices designed to make us feel we can't go an hour without them. But my daily practice takes me into worlds that are far more interesting precisely because they aren't manufactured. And as beautiful as nature is, the spaces of meditation can be even more so—like traveling back to the source, where all glorious things originate and exist in their pure essence.

Sometimes there's a sense of flows and currents; they may carry me or simply move around me. I don't often see colors, but when I do, the light within them is different from the color spectrum that our eyes register. Sounds are more common for me. They may linger in the background, unnoticed, unless I attune to them, at which point they take me higher and deeper into a rarefied version of serene expanse.

Quiet, stillness and silence look empty only at first. The secret is that they teem with qualities that come to light the quieter I become. It's not magic. It's right there, waiting to be found and entered.

a meditation

Many meditators learn to return to the in and out of their own breathing. My method—something I learned early on—draws attention instead to subtle qualities of light, sound and vibration, inviting awareness to shift from the physical toward the more inner landscapes.

A collection of qualities can linger for a while during a phase of my sit, then of their own accord flow into a new constellation of qualities. No session is one hundred percent identical to another, even if many of the same qualities are there.

I can't transmit an actual meditation experience. However, here's a little study in how the qualities came and went one time.

∾

My eyes gently close. I feel the weight of my body, seated, upright, poised.

A near-immediate descent of stillness, quiet, lush darkness.

It calms the body, relaxes the mind. My consciousness spreads.

From the center begins a slow ascension—up, in a continuous circular flow.

Meanwhile, on the periphery, steadiness. A gentle holding.

Lifted up and up, skipping by layers of thought, emotion, streams of collective consciousness. Going high above the currents to an elevated region of cosmic stillness.

Something active. What it is, I can't tell. I wait and watch. And participate in ways I can't yet decipher. A doing that I can't define is underway.

There's warmth in this space. A presence, or presences, much greater than I. Meeting me. Inviting. Welcoming.

Tickling the parts of my consciousness that resonate with it.

It feels good.

Alive. Awake. Fresh. Right.

It continues refining at the exact spot where it has direct access to me. It tousles. Chisels.

Something bigger comes online.

Me. Not me. Of me. Of more than me.

Touched by the forces.

It's beyond a simple stamp.

The forces infuse me. Swirling, spreading, dancing within.

They become part of the texture of my spiritual structure. Weaving.

Permeating into residence.

Stillness deepens further.

Subtler movements. Indistinct, barely recognizable.

Contrasts bring clarity. The will that animates me is but a crude facsimile of this exquisitely pure expression of divine force.

Immeasurably soft.

Breathtakingly strong.

Elegantly precise.

The flavors of this high expression are gifted to me. Imbued into my substance.

It's not assimilation. My presence is neither drained nor diminished.

Combinessence. The coming together on higher planes of divine presence with a certain spiritual substance of me that is capable of functioning here.

An offer, an invitation comes toward me. "Here. This. If you choose."

I respond, go toward it. As I do, I make an offer in return. "Here. Me." Nothing held back. Transparency without guard.

Worldly vision dropped at the outset. Now, otherworldly vision drops away. I no longer see through my lens. I'm taken into the perspective of the presence. Seeing through its eyes.

Its wisdom. Its aspiration. Its natural cosmic landscape. The potentiality of life writ large across time and dimension.

More knowing than the speck of my minor existence.

More compassionate than a parade of religious masters.

More potent than thunder.

Why wouldn't I open to this will?

No thought of harnessing it for my own devices.

Just. Take. Me.

Let me go with you.

What I have is yours.

It always has been.

And always will be.

Whether or not I forget, this constancy of presence is indefatigable.

I say yes.

Again. Again.

Part III
Letting Go

The wound is the place
where the light enters you.

Rumi, Masnavi

UNDOING

messy

I was literally in hot water, which I liked. Emotionally, I was going under. I sputtered out the thought I'd tried to wave away but couldn't make shut up.

"Given what a mess I am, how can you love me?"

Without pause, my best friend responded. "Because I do."

Three simple words far more than words. A soft, fierce force. A crystalline chisel and wooden hammer, tap, tap, tapping at my heart.

We were in a steaming hot tub under tall Oregon pines. Paulina had arrived the night before and was there to deliver balm for my soul. Paulina and I had met five years earlier, and we'd discovered in our friendship a hallowed sisterly love that strangers often mistook for something else. We didn't care. Their assumptions about our devotion to each other were close enough.

I don't recall the details I laid out for her. All I remember is how discombobulated I was. A jumble of unwelcome emotions. Embarrassment, guilt, shame. I was upset and confused about my five-year relationship with Wayne. He and I had moved north from Ashland after he got a new job. Something was very off. His weekend absences, his angry outbursts for no reason—signs I wouldn't decode until later, when I learned about the affair. It compounded my loneliness in a new town 350 miles away from my tight circle of girlfriends.

Paulina listened with a presence that held us both, me in my suspended state of unease, her in equipoise. There were long stretches of silence between comments.

"It doesn't make sense," I said, my voice catching.

"Why not?" she asked.

"Because I'm a train wreck. Pretty unlovable, I'd say." The hot tub churned around us; steam rose into the cool spring air.

As I gave in to feelings of hopelessness about fixing the situation—about fixing me—my eyes watered, and tears dropped from my cheeks into the tub. I didn't want to cry but couldn't help it. The blubbering started; all the ways I must be screwed up tumbled out. I hated not having my shit together. The topper on all my ugliness was my snotty nose and halting speech.

Paulina just listened as I carried on. After I'd gotten it all off my chest, she spoke.

"Honey," she said. "I love the messy parts of you, too. They're part of who you are."

Had I been alone, I would have analyzed the situation, picked out lessons to learn, gotten out of the water and found new projects to restore my sense of worth. But I wasn't alone. Paulina was witnessing it all—my circumstances, my choices, how I was processing them. And somehow her steady presence shifted the spotlight away from the story and toward the cage around my heart. The one I locked away to keep all the messy parts at bay.

The messy parts: this was something I'd never considered about myself, or about others. I'd grown up thinking the deal was to love people for their potential and their accomplishments, despite their flaws. Honor the good and look past the rest. Except when it came to me. I made myself a project, cultivating the good and rooting out the not good. Messy was decidedly not good. A scourge to eradicate.

The logic of perfection as an impossibility didn't matter. I was still driven in that direction, harboring the belief that other people should be too. Wasn't that the point?

Her words cycled over and over in my head, a short loop on replay. They rubbed across the deep grooves in my neural pathways, my well-worn conditioning.

Eventually there was a shift. Something began to loosen. A soft breeze of tender caring rode on the innocence of her words, melting me.

I seemed to be getting help staying still, inside and out, which wasn't my nature. It was calming. Then I was aware of an enveloping around my heart. From there, something gentle sank, slowly, to the inside of it. Circulating, flowing, it made itself at home in the hidden nooks and crannies I'd thought no one would ever touch after I abandoned hope that my father would come to my heart's rescue.

I hadn't asked for this. I didn't want anything or anyone to come inside. It was easier keeping it private because that way, I was in control.

Past a certain point of getting my life together, the mission had become keeping it together. This wasn't part of the plan. It was the antiplan. But here it was. And it felt . . . good. Natural. Maybe even normal.

I had opened without setting out to do it.

It hurt to open. I was wedged so tightly shut that having the door to my heart pried open—not by Paulina's doing but by her steady, reassuring presence—caused an ache. Like moving a leg that had fallen asleep, or reopening a scar that hadn't healed properly, exposing the wound to allow it to heal right this time.

I had to suspend the urge to defend my beliefs—not to her but to myself. I had to open enough to give her words a chance. I was invested in my beliefs; they formed how I saw and operated in the world. Because I trusted her, though, I chose to listen, sincerely. Then I had to go through the discomfort of being a human pressure cooker, letting what she said stand up against the counterarguments of my mind. During the tussle for dominance, both perspectives vying to prevail, I was disoriented. In about ten minutes, out of fogginess came an aha.

She's right. Love just is. Any messiness I am or I create or

I find myself in doesn't have to be cleaned up and swept away for me to be lovable. I don't have to be perfect to be loved. What a concept. No, what a truth.

I became aware of the sound of the wind through the trees and bushes on the outskirts of the property. My shoulders relaxed. We were right where we'd started half an hour earlier, hot water bubbling from the jets and flowing all around us. But everything felt different. I could finally expand rather than hold myself in. When I looked at Paulina through the rising steam, I saw her the way she'd been seeing me all along. Whole, real and beautifully messy.

names

I was given a name at birth that, stereotypically speaking, was part feminine, part masculine. In the South, they do things like that. It was my mother's proud design. She took the first half of her name (Mary Ann) and combined it with her father's name (Thomas). Why? Because she'd promised my grandfather that her next child would be named after him. The result was Mary Thomas—Mary Tom for short.

I didn't mind that it was unique. But when I was old enough to form an opinion of my own, I started to take issue. For one thing, Mary, as she had been portrayed at my Sunday School, seemed unbearably boring. For another, I didn't like the sound of the combined name, Mary Tom. As I grew older, I found hearing it out loud irritating. Fingernails on a chalkboard. By thirty, I was done. I wanted change. But to what?

A friend in Ashland—in an interesting twist, her name was Mary—knew I was ruminating. One day over coffee, she looked across the table and said, "I keep hearing Kira for you." Apparently, she'd been pondering it, too.

I'd never heard that name. Kyra Sedgwick was nowhere on my radar, and Keira Knightley was still a child.

"What's it mean?" I asked.

"I don't know," she said. "I just keep hearing it for you."

I researched baby names at our local bookstore, Bloomsbury. One handbook suggested that the name Kira originated from Cyrus the Great. It had also been popular among Russian women two generations earlier. To my ear, Kira suggested a combination: regal and elfin. I didn't act on Mary's suggestion right away. I simply let it linger in the back of my mind.

A month or so later, I was sitting in the opening circle of a women's workshop in Mill Valley, California. Each woman shared her name and why she was there, and when it was my turn, I introduced myself with my birth name. No sooner had I finished than I got an idea: These people don't know me from Adam. Any name I make up on the spot will be as easy as the next for them to remember.

Before we stood, I raised my hand to speak again.

"If you don't mind, I want to be called a different name. Can you please call me Kira?"

No one flinched. They were excited for me to use the weekend as an experiment. For the next three days, that's who I was.

Every time they said "Kira," I heard proverbial bells ring. It felt so . . . right. As if the name had found the home it was looking for, too.

That's how the reshaping of my label, my name, came to be. I knew I wanted something I liked and that reflected something of my true nature. I didn't orchestrate a search mission.

There was no project with planned steps. I barely lifted a finger. The perfect-for-me answer came through the voice in a friend's head. All I had done was listen to her.

Whether Kira found me or I found it doesn't matter. The change has been delightful. It suits me. There are so many things in life we can't change; names we can. Why tote around a label I don't like? There's no question my parents would have preferred I stick with the name they gave me, but they respected my choice and did their best to understand why it mattered to me.

These days, I no longer flinch at Mary Tom. Family slips up (occasionally they use it to make a point). Friends and colleagues who knew me from school or the early days of my career make valiant efforts, but I know it's not natural to refer to someone by a new first name after you knew them by another. When I hear Mary Tom spoken now, the name is endearing, like rediscovering a long-lost doll from youth and appreciating a moment of sentimental fondness.

I used to put both names to the test with people I was just getting to know. I'd ask, "Which of these is more me?" Kira won every time.

It is said that in Sanskrit, words are not mere symbols. Words are power because they are also the very essence of the object they depict. That's close to how I experience my chosen name. Its vibrational frequency harmonizes with who I know myself to be. Part pixie, part queen. Light combined with sharp clarity. Mysterious and approachable. And more range yet to be discovered and tapped.

stowaway

I am a stowaway on a ship of women. How could they possibly deem me one of them? They move with grace and power, their feminine presence in sharp relief, magnificent and unashamed. I watch them from the shadows of my own guardedness, certain they'll discover I don't belong. These women lead with their sexuality and sensuality—aspects of myself I've learned to muffle, out of habit and protection. We're gathered in an elegant Mill Valley home, fifteen of us, for what they call a workshop, though there are no notebooks, no lectures, no techniques to master. Just women, music and something they call "the rite." The returnees know what's coming. I know only that I'm an impostor among goddesses.

It wasn't always this way. In yellowing family albums, there's a different girl—two, three, four years old—with soft eyes and an undemanding presence, content to watch the world unfold at its own pace. In his stories, my father always described me as sweet, quietly observant. But that softness began dissolving when I became a competitive athlete. I fancied myself the next Chris Evert, whose steely concentration earned her international titles and the nickname "the Ice

Maiden." My good grades came through determination. And New York? New York demanded armor.

When I arrived in the city after college, I was no longer in a small town, where I could move about without care. In the grit of 1980s New York, I needed new behaviors. While walking from my apartment on East 66th to Midtown on my first day of work, I naively expected to make eye contact with passersby. I quickly learned that's not how New Yorkers do it. Within weeks, I looked past strangers, made sidesteps and quick turns, caught crossing lights, avoided alleys. On the subway platform, I jockeyed for position, never getting caught when the doors closed. That was the stuff of very bad dreams. Threats were real.

One misty weekend morning while jogging in Central Park, I rounded the reservoir to find teenage boys waiting. When one grabbed my right buttock, I sprinted away to their laughter. Months later, I caught a pickpocket reaching inside my friend's purse at a street fair. I yanked the thief's wrist back and snarled, "Get out of here!" Fifteen years after leaving New York, I could finally drape my pocketbook over a restaurant chair and trust it would be there when the meal was done.

Self-protection became a package deal; I guarded not just my physical safety, but also my emotions, my career, my very essence. Softness? Openness? Receptivity? I hoisted those up toward the top of the danger list. It took energy and practice to garrison against them, and I became a seasoned expert.

In Mill Valley, I watched as the first woman slipped away to prepare for her rite. She returned in flowing clothes, radiant.

The furniture had been pushed aside for our circle, and the three-part pattern emerged: reflections from the group, then music, then more reflections. Words, sound, words. Movement was optional. So were clothes.

I listened in awe and watched in wonder for three full days. Each woman was her own brand of exquisite. She could be still, then moving; silent, then screaming. She swayed, jerked, flowed, and sometimes collapsed to the floor. When the sound and movement concluded, the women brought her succulent fruit, which she relished as if tasting for the first time.

It surprised me how much I knew about these women despite just having met them. Intuition wasn't new to me, but this was an octave higher. During the reflections, I saw exactly who they were behind the veneer. Actually, we all bore witness with penetrating vision, seeing qualities in each participant that she'd never recognized in herself. Our collective words seemed to float on gossamer wings straight into the heart of each woman during her rite.

Woman after woman passed through an invisible portal and emerged changed in some mysterious way, emptied then filled, savoring the spoils of surrender. By the time my turn came, second to last, my anticipation had built to a nearly unbearable level.

I ducked into the changing room to slide into the burgundy velvet dress I'd brought. Standing before the women, I braced for scrutiny but was fed something else entirely.

"Kira," the first woman to speak said, "I honor your tenderness of heart, and your steely strength. I honor the androgyny and the way you decorate it. There's a pristineness of light. It's very refined." The words landed with surprising truth. A cascade of vision spilled over me as each woman shared what she saw. They captured an essence of my nature that I already knew, or one that I was close to knowing.

The small gallery of women fell quiet. Pat Metheny's music filled the room. My left hand started shimmying—a jazz hand, moving of its own accord. No message from brain to muscle, just pure energy pulsing through me as the first song, "Dream of the Return," played through loudspeakers. Deep, animal screams tore from my throat, followed by moments of breathtaking stillness.

The rite gently transported me to the other side of a threshold and then back again, over and over. It immersed me in a lush sensory world that I usually walled off. I felt stirred, moved, melted, dissolved, sensuous, unguarded and receptive.

When it ended, I found myself in total serenity. Naked and still. Nothing to do. Nothing to change. Not even anything to wonder about. My perpetual curiosity lay quiet.

I simply am.

I became an initiate into the waters of the unbridled feminine as a force of transformation. In those waters, something magnificent in me—and in every other woman—was met by something even bigger from beyond the material world. Some call it the divine feminine, though I don't think the label matters one iota. The thing is to open to it, engage with it, meet it on its own terms. For me, that meant suspending habit. If

I'd seen and felt from my ordinary way of being, I would have held tight to safety and missed the grander opportunity.

Our three days as a small, tight community of women were luscious with dancing, laughter, tears, rites, and connection. We all gave, and we all received. The way to do the workshop wasn't a doing at all. And it didn't involve merely being present. It was more active than that. Something engaged. A giant yes. Without a hint of control or force.

It made me curious about and welcoming of mysteries as they arrived, unannounced and unmistakable. Seeing that which ordinarily existed behind the veil was a privilege I learned to relish. The more I saw, the more the muscle of vision developed, hence the more I could see. The more I saw, the more I opened.

This wasn't drive. It wasn't might. Still, there was a sense of surging forward. Paving a way. Miraculous things happening with no commanding officer seeing to it that they did. A form of navigation that had been utterly foreign to me until now.

I became a repeater, returning seven times over five years. Rather than training me what to do, the workshop swaddled me and allowed essential facets of my nature to emerge. The gentle creature I'd been as a child came alive in a full-grown woman's body. I was no longer a stowaway; I graduated to part of the crew.

The insights that followed were laden with paradox: what's soft is powerful, and vulnerability is not weakness at all. To be effective on earth and in my reach toward the heavens, I needed two expressions of will, one masculine and one feminine. The first had dominated my life; it was active and outwardly focused, bearing down, pressing in, fueled by drive. The second was nothing like that. It was a yin receptivity that created through attraction rather than force, through opening rather than pushing.

Unremarkable to the eye, revolutionary to the spirit.

hills

Soon after moving to Ashland, Oregon, in the nineties, I happened onto the Pacific Crest National Scenic Trail. It wasn't well marked at my entry, so for several weeks I didn't realize that I was day-hiking through a national treasure.

One morning, I made the thirty-five-minute drive from my condo. It was a straight shot up Interstate 5, then an exit onto a winding road toward the Mt. Ashland Ski Area. All told, it was a four-thousand-foot ascent before I parked my car and laced up my hiking boots. I roamed for two hours as cowbells rang in the distance and I gathered purple and yellow wildflowers. Looking south, I eyed Mount Shasta standing proud. It was my first spring in this new wonderland, and my low-grade worry about finances—I was living on savings without yet knowing how I'd make a living here—dissipated as I walked the land. By the end of the hike, my shoulders were relaxed and I had bouquets for the household. An unusual formation I found on the path made me smile; I liked it so much I dislodged it from its resting place and took it home. My housemate, Anita, was away when I returned. I left it on the kitchen table, took a shower, then headed out to run errands.

Anita and I often sat at that table, chatting about our day, our work, our philosophies and our observations on life. The table was next to sliding glass doors that opened to a small backyard and views of the distant hillsides. When I returned from my errands, I discovered that the souvenir from my hike had been moved from the table to the cement patio outside.

"Why did you put it out there?" I asked.

Anita was renting and I was subletting, so technically she had more say than I did. Nevertheless, I was dumbfounded by her action.

"Do you know what it is?" she asked.

"Look at it. It's a face. Don't you see it?"

"So, you don't know what it is." Her eyes were a bit bigger, and the corners of her mouth were starting to turn up.

"I just think it's cool. I found it on my hike today. So I brought it back."

"It's a cow pie," she said.

"What's a cow pie?"

"It comes from a cow . . . They leave it in the pasture . . . It hardens under the sun . . ."

"Oooh! You mean cow shit?"

"Yes." Full smile.

It hit me why she'd wanted it off the kitchen table. Given

her cleanliness gene, I knew how carefully she must have sanitized the table after my deed.

I had seen a mound of dung as though through the eyes of a child—naively and absent any assumptions, beliefs or assigned meaning. When it came to how I saw myself and my life, it was a completely different story.

⁕

I understand why people say that walking in nature can be meditative. It's quieting, often restorative. But I didn't always experience it that way. As a kid I never hiked; I wanted to be on tennis courts where the competition enlivened me. With an opponent to press against—in practice drills or tournament play—my intensity could be unleashed. The court was a stage where I learned strategy, mathematical dimension and mental fortitude. I sought the type of rigor where the satisfaction of release comes from muscles and mind working together, driving the ball, plotting the win or at least improving the stroke. The idea of stilling my mind? That would have seemed ridiculous. I needed the mind, turned on and focused, to achieve what I wanted.

The tide turned in Ashland.

I started hiking for the exercise, but before long I pulled on my boots for a different reason—to escape myself. More specifically, to get out from under the voices in my head and their relentless loop of doom and gloom: You screwed up. What were you thinking? You're not the kind of person who can make a living if you're not an employee. It was a mistake to move to a town where you have no network, no job, no track record to back you. You'll burn through your savings before this situation gets righted.

In retrospect, I was flailing because I'd chosen to extract myself from invisible structures I'd relied on all my life, without new structures to take their place. It was a terrifying limbo.

Hiking had a way of pulling me up out of the morass. In fact, it's where an unforced practice of gratitude started to take hold.

As I took stock, I began to see things differently.

I've got sixteen thousand dollars in the bank. If I'm frugal, it will last seven months. I'm stumped about how to make a living here; even the PhDs in town are pumping gas. Wait—I'm healthy. I can walk this trail pain free. The air is crisp and fresh. The sun is glorious. Gliding along on this trail feels amazing. My doomsday scenario isn't a foregone conclusion. I've met new people who are kind and genuinely want to help me. I have a roof over my head.

I didn't know how it worked, only that it worked. I wasn't doing creative visualization or positive thinking. I was merely letting the cycles of thought run their course. Walking itself produced a release valve—spin up the thoughts, circulate them, let them gain steam, then allow them to release themselves out the hatch. Once that switch was flicked and they shot out, it was as if they'd never held sway. My mind calmed, my heart settled. The reprieve I needed at that instant.

My view might be off, and time changes things anyway.

I never brought home another cow pie. And I rarely left the mountain with a big idea, a thunderbolt solution to a problem. Rather, I was building a new perspective, one that wasn't locked into a lifestyle of safety and security. The beliefs I unconsciously held with tenacious certitude were getting dislodged, and thank goodness for that. When it was too uncomfortable, too unnerving, I headed for the hills. Walking in silence with only the breeze, the birds, the cowbells—it revealed a new-to-me landscape where my psyche exhaled to expand into a new resting place.

This new standpoint, reinforced over and over, week after week, was the bridge that allowed me to cross over to the life I wanted to create—a life of friendships, creativity, inspiration, meaningful contribution and personal autonomy. The gradual unfolding didn't happen because of a plan I carefully laid out, but because I walked away from what I thought I knew about reality and how life should work.

the Pink House

"TAKE IT ALL down," the stager said, gesturing at the walls that held fourteen years of carefully curated art. "Every piece. And those curtains, rods and all."

I gripped my notepad tighter. This was supposed to be about selling a house; why did it feel like dismantling a life? At least I'd given myself a pep talk yesterday. I was braced, if not entirely ready.

Jason, a stout, well-spoken man with a background in set design, moved through my home with swift certainty. My real estate agent, Sam, said he was the best she'd come across, and I could see why. He formed instant, decisive impressions from the moment he stepped inside. I scribbled notes as he rattled off his vision.

"You need a neutral white," he said when we were in the living room. "Most important change right here. And carry it through to the dining room."

Check.

"That chandelier has to go. It's dated and—see there?—cracked. Replace it with something modern, but not too modern. Has to suit the house's character."

I never minded the chandelier. But okay.

"And all the curtains in every room, including the bedroom, need to go."

"What?" The word escaped me before I could stop it. The windows would be naked.

Jason's eyes lit up. It was as if he'd been waiting for someone to challenge him. "Look at all this natural light you're hiding. August in Portland? Golden sunshine streaming in? That's what sells houses. Let it pour through those windows."

He had a point.

"For the exterior, slate gray with cream trim. Perfect for a stucco English cottage." He rattled off the paint numbers with practiced ease.

That could be gorgeous, I thought, already picturing the transformation. It would mark the end of an era that began in the 1940s, when the original owners first made their mark on this house. They had painted it pink and surrounded it with a garden that echoed their choice—pink azaleas nodding in spring breezes, pink rosebushes scattered in the backyard, pink blossoms drifting from the two plum trees that stood sentinel on the parking strip. When I first saw the house, I'd found the color odd but somehow endearing. The paint job itself was solid, so I'd left it, and over the years, it had simply become known as the Pink House. No one ever needed directions to my place. I just said, "You know, the Pink House," and everyone did. Now it was ready for its next chapter, just as I was.

"Take down all paintings and photos. The walls should be blank."

Stark, but I was catching on to the appeal of Jason's blank slate. His singular goal was maximizing sale price by maximizing appeal, and his formula was simple: strip away, clear out, let go. In every room, he detailed what needed to go. To showcase the excellent bones of the house, less was more. Taken together, his suggestions clicked into place.

I smiled at Sam when Jason left. "You were right. He's good."

Sam smiled knowingly and nodded. We compared notes and agreed on everything. A few days later, I hired a contractor who specialized in preparing homes for sale. His team took care of paint and minor repairs. The Saturday before the house went on the market, the three of us—Sam, my husband, and I—rearranged every room. The piano had already been sold and taken away. Dated furniture had been put in storage, and would remain there until I had time to off-load it.

I wouldn't have removed so much without Jason's prodding. But once it was gone, I felt as though I'd moved into a new home. Why had I never thought to do this before? Clearing it out created an airiness that showed off the architecture. And it didn't just lighten the house. It lightened me up, too. Emptier simply felt better.

It didn't escape me that fourteen years earlier, when I first toured the house, it was empty, not staged. I made an offer, we negotiated a bit, and I moved in with next to no belongings. I took my time turning the house into a little haven, adding the sea-blue velvet couch, the wide reading chair, the black-and-white zebra rug, and the various plants on stands. Ultimately, I ended up with far more than I needed. More than I wanted. More than what suited who I was to become.

Why, I wondered, do I fight emptiness? During meditation, emptiness is gold. When my mind jabbers it jams the works, whereas an empty mind can go places. It can lift off and soar. A quiet mind is the price of admission to a high-quality meditation.

Emptying my mind was far from natural when I started meditating. My thoughts were quite content to hang around after I closed my eyes. They'd cycle through lists. Conversations. Things I wanted. Things I'd messed up.

Who am I if I don't have these thoughts anymore?

My brain's function was such a big part of my identity. I'd worked hard to be smart, dependable, capable. The person you'd want nearby in an emergency. It was unfathomable that I would exist without the stream of thoughts; they reminded me I was alive. Would sacrificing my internal dialogue in hopes it would yield something better be worth it? I settled for an unconscious bargain: seek relief from negative thoughts but keep the good ones. No need to throw the baby out with the bathwater.

Sometimes I need others to show me what's possible. Two

teachers, one spiritual and one atheist, from two different eras of my life, touted the same principle: we often see more clearly in others what we struggle to recognize in ourselves. Jason saw what my house needed; he saw the power of emptiness, the beauty in bare walls, the grace in absence. Watching him move through my rooms, decisive and clear-eyed, I wondered if he lived this way himself, or if, like me, he needed outside eyes to see his own attachments.

The genuine desire for silence—true emptiness, not just selective clearing—came slowly. In meditation, as in my home, I had to taste the possibility before I could want it fully. Now, having experienced that less is more, it's become a preference that grows stronger with practice. If I died tomorrow, my survivors would find little to clear away. Like my meditation practice, my living space is constantly being winnowed down to what matters most.

There ought to be a verb that captures this intentional release, this practiced letting go. *Winnow* comes closest— remove the chaff from the grain, eliminate the excess to find the essence. Yes, something is lost. The form changes. What was here will be gone. But the release itself becomes a kind of grace, an invitation to what's next. It may seem strange to approach loss with enthusiasm, but that's exactly what meditation is teaching me: the joy in letting go and the regeneration that comes with it.

devotion

For some reason, the phrase "give up" rattled around in my head one weekend while I was in the midst of writing this book. I found it interesting because of how out of place it was. I wasn't contemplating giving up on anything in my life. Nevertheless, the phrase stuck like Velcro, affixed to its own marquee. Every so often, it flashed to grab my attention.

So, I chose not to give up on it. Slow down, take a breath, take a look. What's it doing there?

As soon as I paused and looked, I had to smile. One definition of "give up" is "to quit." Shrug one's shoulders and walk away. Throw in the towel. Let it be.

Taken literally, it is giving, an offering, toward the sky: up. Presumably, it is directed to someone or something above. Instead of quitting, it could be praying. Instead of resignation, it could be aspiration.

It could be devotion.

That's a word I heard all through childhood. It always

bugged me. For one thing, the notion made no sense. How can you be devoted if it's not to a person? For another, it was my mother who said it. When she did, it meant she wanted space for herself. She asked us—actually, begged us—to leave her alone for a few minutes every day.

"So I can do my devotions," she'd say.

Each month, a small book arrived in the mail. Her daily devotions. One page per day. All she wanted was a few quiet minutes alone every day to read and reflect. She had the discipline and the desire.

Just not the family that would honor her impulse.

At best, we did it begrudgingly. I told myself that if I didn't understand that book, or what she did with her time alone, then this ritual called devotions wasn't valid. The fact was, I didn't approve of her withdrawing to seek solitude. I could feel her pull away from all of us in her attempt to nurture herself and her unique brand of spirituality. When that happened, my siblings and I exercised our primary childhood power. We got noisy. The brats in us didn't think Mom deserved a break from her job as mom.

In retrospect, I wish she hadn't had to fight so hard to claim space and time for the one thing that was hers alone. Was it really too much to ask us to move to a different room and shut up for fifteen minutes? That's all she wanted, merely enough time to read a page from the book, close her eyes and contemplate what she'd read as she nestled in the wingback chair with the ottoman, on which she could finally rest her feet.

Like my mother, I found a brand of spirituality that suits me. It's not the kind one finds in a church or mosque. I sought for decades and finally found a path to match my appetite. Along the way I discovered devotion. Not as a formula. Not as a method or practice. But as an offering that is never-ending, that remains operational in the background as life's events unfold.

Like my mother, I'm in a household where my spiritual path is neither shared nor fully understood. But unlike her, I'm graced with the gift of silence when I sit to meditate. My husband moves quietly about the house if he knows I'm in the meditation room.

My own room. A silent house. Time alone. I never take these for granted. Though my husband doesn't fully understand what I do when I'm doing it, he honors how important it is to me. He sacrifices through small inconveniences on my behalf.

So that I can give, up.

RESTING

imperial

After a summer course at my meditation school, I made a simple decision that blew up in my face: I invited one of the students to a follow-up weekend intensive at my home, without first asking the three friends who'd helped plan it. I thought I was being inclusive. They thought it was time for an intervention. Looking back, I can see they were right.

The retreat at the school had hit all the right notes. Deep states of stillness. Activation of new awareness. Greater access to spiritual forces above. And meaningful connections with other meditation students. During the eight-hour drive home, I considered how to ground my new learning into action. One idea was already in motion. A handful of us from Oregon and Washington would meet at my home for a weekend of practices. We'd already sketched out a plan; we just needed to pick dates.

In my meditation school, practices happen solo or with partners—two or more at a time. As we explore spaces of consciousness together, being playful is often the key, similar to driving. With a new-to-you car, you start awkward, checking mirrors and adjusting seats. Gradually, the car becomes an extension of you. You stop thinking about driving and just drive.

In a partner practice, it's as if you're joined by a passenger and you take a road trip together. You and the passenger might use different words to describe what you see, but you're experiencing the same journey. The landscape unfolds for you both. Moreover, inner landscapes become more visible, and they're often light-years brighter than your personality or that of your companion.

My instinct is always to include people, to widen the circle when I can. Maybe it's generosity. Maybe it's childhood memories of not being invited to play. Either way, it's been a habit to extend the invitation first, ask questions later.

So, I went ahead and invited Wenndi from Southern California, then casually dropped the news in an email to the others:

Hi everyone,

Good news: Wenndi can join us for the upcoming intensive in June. She'll be flying in Friday night.

Question: What do you all prefer on Monday . . . going through the evening, spending the night and departing Tuesday, or wrapping up end of day Monday so people can leave after an early dinner?

Love,

K

I sat back, pleased with myself, imagining how much better this would be with five instead of four.

The response came the next day: Could we have a planning call? Just the original four of us.

Great idea, I thought.

That one hour changed my life.

The call began normally, with quick hellos, settling into silence, attuning to the space. Then Paulina spoke.

"Before we plan the weekend, there's something else we need to cover."

"Sure," I said, missing whatever signals they'd telegraphed.

"You invited Wenndi without checking with us first."

"Yeah, sorry about that. I probably should have." A lame apology that barely qualified as one.

"We all love Wenndi, but that's not the point. The four of us made plans together, and you made a command decision to change them."

Right, I thought. So what? Not really a big deal.

"Why did you do that?"

"Well, I figured we all like her."

"We do."

"And since it's at my house and I'm hosting, I thought I could make that call."

"Honey," Paulina said, her voice warm with care, "that's why we wanted to have this call." Interesting—she didn't see this as a simple oversight. If she had, she would've called alone to sort it out. I squirmed.

"Look, I can disinvite her. It'll be awkward, but she'll understand. I'll say I jumped the gun." Easy fix. Let's move on.

"Slow down. Did you actually forget to check with us? Look deeper. Where did that decision come from?"

I went quiet, searching for my original motivation.

"I was telling Wenndi about our plans. She said it sounded great, that she'd love to come. I figured you'd all say yes, anyway, so I went ahead and invited her on the spot." As I spoke, I reconnected with my enthusiasm for including her, all she'd bring to our weekend.

"We might have said yes, but that's not the real issue. Did you make a unilateral decision?"

"Yes." Put that way, I couldn't miss it. Hadn't I already admitted it in so many words?

"You said you think you get to make the decision. What part of you thinks it has that right, just because you're hosting?"

Discomfort crept in. Paulina was circling something I couldn't quite see. And whatever it was, it had required all three of them on this call. That much I understood.

Then David spoke. "It's not the first time. I've seen you do things like this before." He could be disarmingly direct, and his accusation put me off kilter. But it carried no blame. In my family, confrontations like this were dogfights. Here, there was no malice.

"What do you mean? We haven't done a weekend like this before."

"You're deciding for you. Only you. Not with anyone else in mind. You want it your way. That's normal enough, but here's what you need to see: you don't want anyone to know you do it. You hide it. You maintain a secret world where Kira is queen. She's ruthless, while you're clueless."

Gulp. This was no surface scratch. David had plunged us into deep water, forcing me to see myself through his eyes.

"When someone challenges you, you spin it. You put together a convenient story. It has nothing to do with what really drives you. It's so automatic, you probably don't know you're doing it."

I didn't. But with him putting his finger on it, I sort of did.

The last person to speak was Jen. "Kira, we're here because we love you. We care about your process. This is coming up for a reason. We want to support you in seeing it. It's time."

It was an intervention, and I was its subject.

If the three of them hadn't enveloped me in just the way they did, I would have tried manipulation. Played up my innocence, then, after hanging up, nursed my indignation. Three things saved me.

First, I'd seen other spiritual seekers hit this wall before, had seen the resistance that comes when the truth is revealed and someone isn't ready to see it. Those stories usually ended badly. I refused to squander a magical moment wrapped in a shit sandwich.

Second, I'm a Scorpio. Intensity is like air. Though the situation was out of my control, it gave me a perverted sense of satisfaction.

Third, I had Jen, David and Paulina fiercely rooting for me. They weren't trying to make me better behaved. They were showing me a force inside me that steamrolled people in my way. A force that maintained an invisible divide between them and me. A force that would forever impede the spiritual connections I craved—unless I could see it clearly.

They must have expected me to balk. Instead, I squirmed but didn't recoil.

"Tell me more," I said. "When else? What else did I do? I believe you, but I'm drawing a blank."

The examples poured out. They came prepared, not armed. I listened like a blind woman learning to see through others' eyes. Their stories painted a vivid picture of my choices, my cloaks, my pretexts. As they walked me through each situation, I felt a strange alertness. Not fight or flight—but earnest curiosity.

It was as though I were watching the turning point of my own movie, knowing the protagonist's next choice would dictate the story's ending. She sounds calm; is it a ruse? Why hasn't she lashed out yet? Isn't this too much tension for one person to hold?

The thing was, I wasn't holding the tension alone.

My friends formed an outer container with their fierce care, while I created an inner one. At my core, where I rattled, I applied persistent gentle pressure. This kept the energy moving so it wouldn't implode. Too much restraint and the rattle would recede, taking with it the refined level of awakeness needed to register the presence of a pattern. Too little restraint and the rattle would randomly strike anything in its path.

Like every major character in a story, this persona deserved a name. Before the intervention was over, I decided to call her my Imperial Self—it fit her above-it-all attitude of entitlement. She's hardwired; she'll never completely disappear. But seeing the Imperial Self for what she is makes me more aware when she's about to run roughshod. From that vantage point, I can make an honest choice.

For forty-five minutes, I was double-wrapped. No one got hurt. As uncomfortable as it was, I stayed present. Finally, I said, "I see what you're seeing. Thank you. It's just . . ." I choked up, my heart in chaos. "Knowing the gory details, I can't believe you still love the person who did those things. I know you do. It's hard to let that in."

My protective wall had gone weak-kneed. My friends' sustained warmth melted my defenses. It hurt so good.

Full sobs. Silence on their end. Nose-blowing. Then sniffles.

"Thank you," I whispered again.

"Of course. You're welcome." All in a day's ferocious love.

rest

"I'M CALLING TO rest on you."

"Okay," I said. I thought she was using East Coast slang.

"Is there anything in particular you want?" I asked.

"No," my friend replied. "Just talking. I need a place to rest. It's been hard the last few days."

"So, just talking will do it for you?"

"Yeah."

"Okay, I can do that."

It was the easiest thing in the world to give her; no effort or doing on my part. I didn't even have to think about it because it was so natural. She was calling from across the country, where her new community wasn't exactly welcoming her with open arms. I'd thought she just needed a friendly voice, someone to share stories and take her mind off her troubles. Instead, she taught me about a different kind of holding.

Resting goes far beyond listening and sharing. It's a form

of nonphysical holding so someone can let go for a moment, relax, not have to uphold themselves all by themselves. Their body of energy rests on another for a stretch of time, whether the two people are in the same room or oceans apart.

We rest on each other. Full stop.

It's been said that all strong leaders (usually in reference to men) have a great woman behind them. Their partners aren't just whipping up meals, dealing with the kids and arranging vacations. Even CEOs who aren't emotionally expressive or needy—and many aren't—often have spouses who provide an emotional resting place, often nonverbally.

This invisible architecture of support takes different shapes. I think of a university president whose weekly commitments extended into evenings and weekends for dinners and community-building events. Most presidents have a spouse to help bear that load. She knew when she accepted the job that she'd be doing it from a slight disadvantage—she didn't have a partner. Instead of tapping her closest staff to fill that void, she consciously chose to rest on her brother and other family members. They were her weekly touchstones, the people she could just be with.

Not everyone has the instinct or training to rest on another without causing strain. I've known people who wear me down with their neediness, exhausting me. Their situation, as they share it, takes me down with them. That's not resting; it's dumping. By contrast, my friends can be blue, frustrated or disappointed as they rest on me without it demanding anything extra.

Since that conversation with my friend, I've noticed that there are people I can rest on without naming it or even asking. And there are those who, though they have many beautiful traits, don't have that rest-on-able quality. I've also noticed that it feels great to have someone rest on me when they're brilliant at holding themselves. Why? Because it marks the moment when they're at their own edge. They've pushed their limit. They don't need to be saved in any way. They just need a respite. A bit of time to regroup and gather their energy back up.

I think about all the ways my friend and I have learned to rest on each other across distance and time. We all need people to rest on. Sometimes it's our spouses and elders; sometimes it's the friend who picks up the phone and knows exactly what we mean when we say, "I just need to rest."

EMPTYING

gone then gone

Two days before my father died, my mother cracked a joke about him jumping out of bed to answer the doorbell when his hospice nurse arrived. He'd have to do it because she and I were collapsed in exhaustion on the floor. I laughed until I cried. Gallows humor, I finally conceded, helps us survive moments that are otherwise devastating. What I didn't know yet was that death would teach me more about my father than life ever had.

After he died, we did as he wished and scattered his ashes near his favorite holes at his golf club. He was so beloved there that the staff looked the other way on that sunny July morning as we made our rounds on the back nine. It felt right that his final resting place involved a little rule-bending—it had been the way he lived.

Seven months earlier, when my older sister called to tell me the diagnosis, my dad and I were barely speaking. Just forced conversations on birthdays and holidays. I was at work and had to step out of a meeting to take her call. The news landed flat as a fact.

"Are they sure?" I asked.

"Yeah," Elizabeth replied. "They already saw a specialist."

"What were his symptoms?"

She explained the pain he had, the tests they ran. The conclusion.

"Can they operate?"

"No. Something about where the cancer is."

Okay, I thought.

"How long did they give him?"

"They said six months to a year."

A world without him in a year. Hard to fathom. Nevertheless, my low-grade anger toward him buffered the shock. Earlier, when my parents reversed their position on a family conflict that had split us all apart, I couldn't follow their reasoning and violently disagreed. I resigned as executor of their will—partly out of spite but mostly cold logic: you don't hire a contractor who can't understand your vision. How could I carry out their final wishes when I'd lost the thread of how they saw the world? Let my older sister take that role.

The medical crisis forced a reckoning. Time called my bluff, and Dad and I began speaking again, carefully steering around the family divide. I flew from Oregon to Georgia with my husband-to-be, and I watched him fall in love with my parents—it was his first time meeting them. My father, an avid athlete, didn't let pancreatic cancer cut into his practice time or golf rounds. They went together, the golfer and the nongolfer, out to the golf club. Dad's conversational style and questions that cut straight to the mechanics of things were entertaining and endearing to almost everyone, and especially to my husband-to-be. The outing gave him a glimmer of what it might have been like to pursue a sport, just father and son.

When they returned after their round, my father wasted no time sharing what he'd learned on the golf course.

"It sounds like they're going to get married," Dad said to Mom. Then he turned to the two of us. "Well, you'd better hurry up if you want me there," he said—not to nudge or pressure, but simply to state the bittersweet obvious.

My husband-to-be asked if I wanted a shotgun wedding to accommodate my father's inescapable timing. No, I said. I had done a lot of things because of my father in this life. Getting married before I was ready wouldn't be one of them.

Our reunion accomplished what it needed to. We were speaking and, more importantly, caring. His life continued with the rhythms he knew so well—small familiar acts he kept up as best he could—until pain eventually overtook him. When hospice care began, my siblings and I took turns helping Mom—the physical and emotional demands had become too much for her alone. Somehow, without discussion, we all knew the final shift would be mine. Not because of any rotation schedule, but because something in my nature lent itself to the role of final usher. I flew east on a one-way ticket. He passed three weeks later.

I learned that death can be hard work. For everyone. Two days before he died, I was in his bedroom with him all night, watching his uneven, labored breathing. A breath in, a breath out, then stillness that stretched twice as long. Each new breath brought a little shake and startle. Countless times I thought I'd witnessed his last, only to hear air flowing back in.

He was in pain, too. His body made involuntary movements, writhing. Mom and I were following the hospice nurse's instructions regarding medication timing and dosage; it wasn't enough to take the edge off. We could go higher, but I was afraid to overdo it, concerned the painkillers would take him out. Mom was upstairs sleeping, and I didn't want to wake her; she needed rest.

As the night wore on, I urged him to let go. He was mildly delusional, but I spoke as if he could hear me and comprehend what I said. "It's okay, Dad. You can relax. There's no need to fight for your life anymore. You can go." But his body, and part of his mind, was in full revolt against the inevitable. At 4:00 a.m., I called our hospice provider and asked them to send a nurse. Mom appeared in the doorway of the main bedroom. She'd been sleeping in another room ever since Dad's sleep turned erratic, making it hard for her to get a good night's rest. She wanted to see how we were doing. I told her about the night, about calling for hospice reinforcements.

The nurse arrived before dawn. She wasn't timid about upping the morphine dose. He needed it, she said.

He died twenty-three hours later.

Mom was with him at the end, lying beside him, singing softly. After he was gone, she stayed for two more hours, just the two of them. Then she came to my bedroom to let me know. It was over.

I got up, pulled on yesterday's clothes and pattered downstairs. I wasn't glad he'd died, but I was glad for all of us that the ordeal was over. I wanted to see his body, the residual physicality, now that my father had left it. I entered my parents' bedroom. Mom followed. The bed was to the right of the door. He was lying on his back, hands resting outside the covers at midtorso, eyes closed, mouth slightly open. His expression took me by surprise. Pure peace, an epic contrast to the preceding days, when he'd grimaced in pain, his body struggling to prolong life, as if longer were somehow better. Now he looked at ease, as though he'd finally let go. It soothed me to see it.

Then I became aware of the room itself, filled with peace, too. It wasn't an aura I observed from outside, but one I stood within. The bedroom was still the bedroom, but also a chamber, filled to the brim, completely infused. I'd never sensed anything like it. While I rarely speak of heaven, this felt like flavors of what heaven must surely be. A nonhuman presence imbued everything with grace. It was stable, not fleeting, as though it had settled in for a stay.

I marveled. This is what came for him. This is what ushered him away. Why would anyone fight this? It bore no resemblance to the sharpness of the grim reaper. Quite the opposite. This was caring at an order of magnitude that took my breath away. I wanted to bottle it, share it. Couldn't we always be embraced like this, instead of saving it for death?

ॐ

Later that morning, we tended to necessary details. Calls to family. Calls to our hospice provider and the morgue. Mom wanted a celebration of life, not a memorial, and began planning the program. When she mentioned bagpipes, I felt a flash of joy. Dad had loved the scene from *The Music Man* with "Seventy-Six Trombones." He would parade around like a jacked-up band leader, pumping his knees high and swinging his elbows wide.

Many spiritual traditions have rituals for the deceased. Mine centers on the spirit of the departed, rather than the remains of their body, and it involves reading to the newly dead. The script I use comes from an audio course called *Death: The Great Journey*, created by Samuel Sagan. Although it is a modern, non-religious text, it's easy to see in it parallels to *The Bardo Thödol*—better known in the West as *The Tibetan Book of the Dead*.

For those I love, I read to help them adjust to their new situation. I can't figure it out for them, but I can serve as a reference point in their passage toward the light beyond. If the way isn't immediately clear, I can help them find it.

This is a privilege. I've done it for friends who've passed, and each time I learn something special about the essence of their being—qualities that were less visible during their earthbound existence. The protocol is specific: every day, at the same time, I read to them for thirty minutes. Both the act and its impact are profound.

The purpose of reading to my deceased friends and family isn't to keep them around because I don't want to lose them. I do it to lend them a navigational leg up. Help them get their bearings. Loosen any sense of obligation to the world they just left. Point out a particular light that's there for them—the start of a pathway on their new journey as a soul.

The light.

It's not something our physical eyes register, but spirits can sense this frequency once they know to look for it. One simple word—"light"—that manifests in countless forms. As a meditator on a path of vision, I've witnessed it express itself as cool, warm, thin, flowing, dense, white, colors, glowing, piercing, vast, laser-like, refined beyond measure, and on and on. There's a particular light, a source, that, if they catch it and follow it, will make their transition smoother and easier. I'm there to remind them to look and go.

I'd brought the text with me to my parents' home in Thomasville. That afternoon, I selected a spot for reading, a quiet nook by a steepled window on the second floor, well removed from noisy household activities. I liked the way the window reached toward the sky. Before speaking, I tuned in to my father. This process is different from remembering. Rather than relate to his personality, I sensed qualities of his being that were actively present. Literally alive. What stood out was his drive to understand—not just golf swings and circuit designs, but great mysteries of the universe and problems of magnitude that inventors were drawn to. As I connected to his spirit, I could feel the vastness behind that drive. What he'd been able to access while in a body was minuscule compared to what this new dimension offered him. He hadn't wasted any time. He'd started turning over cosmic stones before we met up that afternoon for the first reading.

My father seemed to adjust quickly. He was soaring in no time, feeding his appetite for knowledge and freed from the anguish of a body that had turned on him. I kept reading to him. Daily. I continued the practice when I got home.

Within the first two or three days, I realized that who I was reading to wasn't exactly who I knew as my dad. His presence was bigger, defying role or identity. I was getting to know my father as a spirit—the essence of who he was before he was born and the form he was returning to after death. Joyful. Creative. Magnanimous.

I fell in love with him.

It was hard not to cry in the first few days of reading. I had grief to process and didn't want to put it on him as a soul in early transition, sensitive to the pull of human emotion. It took time before I could contain my emotions without effort. Still, each reading brought pure joy. I was in awe of his being. I could tell he didn't entirely need me to help navigate, though he seemed so enamored with his newfound range that he might have looked right past the light that invited him into higher realms.

This spirit, this magnificent being, was a marvel. I relished every thirty-minute set together. As he transitioned in the direction he was meant to go, his presence grew less and less tangible. A slow and gradual fade. Within three weeks, he was gone. On to the next plateau.

I was elated for him.

And triply sad for myself, bidding him farewell so soon after finally truly knowing him.

jawbreaker

That warm autumn day, I measured my bike ride in miles and speed. A twenty-five-mile loop, and less than ninety minutes to complete it. I knew every turn, every slope, every potential hazard. What I didn't know was the profound cost of fixing my eyes on the wrong thing.

My boyfriend's words from that morning still burned in my ears as I approached the familiar bike-path entrance. "You have a nice body. But it could be better." As in, more like those of his last two girlfriends. They had long, sinewy legs. Mine were long, muscular, and not shaped to his complete liking.

The Cadillac between the entrance and me was moving impossibly slowly. A woman in her seventies or eighties was driving, staring at the road ahead, oblivious to what was happening around her. "What a sleeper," I muttered. Three seconds later, I was airborne.

I thought I had enough speed and upper-body strength to jump the curb. I was wrong. The tip of my chin took the full force of the impact. My hands didn't have time to break any part of the fall.

I barely moved on the concrete, stunned. The reality that I was on the ground seemed impossible. But there I was, and I knew without question that the pressure of my teeth when they snapped shut had broken my jaw. Later, I would learn the technical term: *bilateral condylar fracture*. Well-meaning Samaritans rushed over, looking stupefied by what they'd seen. How can she be conscious? I told them I was fine, I just needed my boyfriend to come pick me up. They kept insisting on an ambulance. When my boyfriend didn't answer my call, I gave in to their urgings.

The X-ray technician at the hospital barely glanced at me—just another oversensitive woman who could afford time off to cycle on a weekday. He adjusted my body roughly, dismissing my muffled sounds of pain. Then he saw the films. His demeanor shifted, eyes widening slightly. She was right after all.

A week later, the surgeon examined the panoramic X-ray. "I wish I'd been there to catch your head as you fell," he said, his voice gentle, his eyes compassionate. He cupped his hands as if catching a weighty bowling ball.

"You'll never be able to eat a sandwich the same way," he continued. "Your teeth won't pierce whatever's in the middle. Your condyles are too thin for surgery. The best we can do is wire your mouth shut for four weeks to relieve some of the trauma in your bones and tissue."

An absolutely terrible prognosis. My body was still in shock, so the news entered my head in cloud form, not as the full reality it was. A decade of complicated jaw and dental work, finally complete, and now this. At least my teeth had survived intact, not a single crack or break. Small mercies.

I no longer buy the idea that everything happens for a reason. When I hear people say it, I sustain my gaze but inside, my eyes roll. I used to tell myself everything happens for a reason to take the sting out and feel as if I had power over situations I didn't have any power over.

Sure, I lost this, but I gained that.

Yeah, it hurt, but look what I learned.

Something good had to be behind something bad.

How I see it now is that not all losses are gains. I've lost people I loved when they passed away or exited my life for other reasons. I really lost them. The memory of them isn't the same as having them with me. Regardless of how much grace accompanied their transition, or how much emotional healing brimmed from their death process, I cannot seek their wisdom or share a meal with them. I'll never get them back. True and final loss. I would not have chosen to let go of them.

How many times have I replayed those three seconds? If someone offered me a do-over, I'd take it in a heartbeat. Not only my body took a hit—so did my pocketbook. High insurance deductibles meant I paid thousands out-of-pocket for emergency-room services, the ambulance ride and doctors' appointments. Since I was in no condition to work, I had to forgo consulting income. The plans I'd hatched for a special foray to South America to learn Spanish came to an abrupt halt. Instead, I remained stateside, pining for a redo of the instant that stopped the clock on the old normal.

The only people I came in contact with were those who naturally understood how to be with me in my shattered state. I rested on them exclusively. I was too fragile to let anyone else inside the house.

For six weeks, I welcomed homemade soups from friends who delivered to my doorstep. Sipping through a straw was the only way I could take in most food. The only solids allowed were scrambled eggs.

Though it was against my grain, I had to surrender to a different mode of being. It turned out to be a crucial passage. While I would still take back the bike accident, I would not reverse the shattering of other things that were part and parcel of it: how I knew myself, how I moved in the world, and the determination, formed as a little girl, that I had to get it together. Though dazed, I was gaining clarity. I hadn't realized how much my consciousness depended on invisible structures—structures I'd started carefully erecting at a young age. The accident sharpened my acuity to discern what I had relied on, and how flimsy it was. The condyle snap broke a spell. What I couldn't have expected was how this inner shift would change the way I worked.

When I was finally ready to fly from my perch back into the world, my career took two welcome turns. A strategic planning retreat with a board of directors was already scheduled. I called my client, certain they'd want to find someone else. How could I facilitate with my jaw wired shut?

"No," he insisted. "We'd prefer to have you."

After discussing modified logistics, I said yes. What I didn't tell him was that I felt stripped bare. My emotional deconstruction, triggered by the accident, had left me defenseless. When the retreat came, I had no choice but to work outside my carefully constructed professional image.

Something unexpected happened. Twice during the day, I saw the board about to dig themselves into a hole. Uncharacteristically, I didn't move to redirect them. I simply observed, stated what I saw, and offered a suggestion. They recovered quickly. After the meeting, an attorney who was also a former city commissioner pulled me aside.

"I've led a lot of meetings and been in rooms with a lot of facilitators, but I've never seen anyone do it like you," he said. "I watched you work, but I can't figure out how you do it."

I couldn't explain that my broken jaw had broken something else, too—my need to manage my professional persona. All I had left was presence, the ability to name what was right under my nose, and the courage to participate without managing the outcome.

As I regained my footing in the professional world, still testing this new way of being, another door opened. A friend and colleague I had met one afternoon in her downtown office was stacking papers before leaving for the day.

"There's someone you need to meet," Carole said as she pulled on her coat. "He's reimagining education in Portland, but he needs a facilitator who can hold space for difficult conversations. I thought of you."

By then my jaw had been unwired, and I was eating solid foods again. The nonprofit leader's vision was ambitious: transform public education by bringing together people who rarely sat at the same table. One meeting led to another, and he offered me a three-quarter-time role. It eased the immediate pressure on my consultancy and opened entirely new doors.

Without leaving the country or the county, I was transported to another culture, where Black, Latino, Asian, and Indigenous American leaders convened with business executives, government officials, foundation directors and educators. Together, they systematically tackled vexing educational disparities. Facilitating their exploration offered some of the most challenging and rewarding moments of my career.

Would I call these two twists my silver linings? Lemonade out of lemons? Not really. I prefer not to muddy the waters, so I break things down this way:

There was an accident. My actions led to it. It came with costs and with grace. Some doors closed and other doors opened. Would I have changed anyway? Eventually, yes. But not necessarily in the same ways.

There are things I will never know for sure. Was the accident a shortcut instead of a detour? Did my will crave something I was denying, causing it to leak out and wreak havoc? I don't need to know these answers. What I do know is that when I felt transparent and raw, it wasn't a miserable sensation. It wasn't the terrible fate I'd imagined. It was emancipation. The energy I'd spent constructing defenses could finally go somewhere else. Without barriers, I could step forward into what was actually there.

stripped

I married late in life, when my foundations felt solid—career established, finances secure, spiritual practice deep and steady. What I sought was the kind of transformation that can emerge only through intimate partnership. The friction that would smooth my rough edges. The mirror that would show me what I couldn't see alone.

I entered marriage with visions common to many: joy, harmony, playfulness, honest communication. These, I expected, would be our foundation in the face of life's inevitable challenges. What I didn't expect was trial by fire with a home remodel that would take over a decade.

Long before the wedding, we'd begun house-hunting. A clean start in a new house made more sense than moving into either of the homes we owned separately. We shared a common sense of aesthetic, hungry for a modern design in a quiet neighborhood. It would be close enough to my husband's job to give him a straight shot to the office. I'd continue running my business from home—part of the lifestyle I'd carefully crafted over years to support both my work and spiritual practice.

The housing market, tighter than it had been in years, frothed with panicked buyers. Prices climbed amidst a razor-thin inventory across the region. We lost out on the homes we bid on. Then along came the ten-year-old house with midcentury design. My husband had noticed it a few years earlier and told himself that if it ever went on the market, he'd buy it. So, we did. It was palatial to me, nearly four thousand square feet, but it passed our "more than good enough" test. With new paint, carpet and appliances, repairs to the wood floor and an updated fireplace wall, it would be a banger starter house for our union.

After we'd been showering for a few months in a "windowless dark cave," my husband surprised me with a proclamation. He didn't want to live in the house without completely redoing both bathrooms. This renovation wouldn't be just for our benefit, he explained, but also for resale value, given the outdated milieu of tan tile. I didn't object to the change, just the timing. I countered that it could be phase two, after we knocked off the list we already had.

Our interior designer was well-versed in the tension couples experience during remodels. She diplomatically inserted this idea: one person might be comfortable with prolonged mayhem, while the other might need stretches without chaos in order to get through it. I fell unapologetically in the latter camp and said so. My husband identified with the former, and insisted it be one broader phase. Moreover, he was unwilling to live in the house while the remodel was underway. Too much dirt and inconvenience.

I relented and we vacated. As the project progressed, his

eye for design kept improving. Let's get new stone for the kitchen island. The decks need new flooring. The foyer will pop with new tile. The cabinet and drawer doors are worn and plain. And . . .

The list grew.

As a result, in the ten years we've owned the house, we've lived there together a mere eighteen months.

Becoming a remodel nomad wasn't the type of change I'd had in mind when I said yes to marriage. I hadn't projected a year of sleeping atop an inflatable bed while my perfectly comfortable queen mattress languished in storage. Nor had I anticipated needing to rent an office to find a quiet spot in which to work. All the ways I'd diligently feathered my home nest and my work spaces dematerialized. The foundation I'd depended on—a welcoming, stable, unrockable sense of home—vanished.

For about a year, we lived at my husband's place; I'd already sold mine. I took advantage of its one strength: proximity to great roads for cycling. When he started inching toward remodeling it so he could sell it, we moved into a rental in a quaint, heavily wooded Portland neighborhood called Multnomah Village. Another midcentury modern home, smaller than ours. When that lease was up, we moved to a rental twenty-five miles north, over the vast Columbia River into Washington state.

Four homes in four years.

I'd never moved that frequently in all my life. Not even

between college dorms. With each move, I felt as if I were being forced into a deeper layer of relinquishment. Whatever I'd given up before wasn't enough. More had to be taken away. My arsenal of comforts shrank. Bathtub. Furniture. Plants. Books. Cozy pillows. It seemed as though an invisible hand was stripping away all the ways I like to rest in a home. It was disrupting. It was disheartening. I wanted to cry. I did cry. I'd worked hard to create conditions that would allow me to thrive. Home was a centerpiece. I had it no more.

I was neither silent nor passive through our remodel morass. My husband, who grew up in a military family, moved every one or two years before he turned eighteen. He'd never put down roots and didn't fully comprehend my predicament. When I delivered a mild ultimatum intended to motivate him—no more trips or outings until we turned our current rental home into a nest—he finally sat up and paid attention.

"What does that mean?" he asked. "What exactly does a 'nest' look like to you?"

I was quick to reply. To me it was obvious.

"We get all the moving boxes out of the family room and into the garage. We set up a place to eat our meals. The kitchen island, from here on out, is for food only. Not files."

"What else?"

"We buy a couch and create a nook where we can sit together and talk or watch a movie. Last but not least, we hang the art."

"That's all?"

"Yep. It doesn't take much."

A month later, we had a nest.

It didn't hold me in quite the same way the Pink House had, but it would do. My nervous system took a comforting in-breath. My body started to relax, and my mind settled down. A few days later, I noticed my awareness was on new and interesting things because it wasn't unconsciously prepping for the next event that would unmoor me. This alone freed up tremendous mental and emotional space. Feeling more balance internally, I was naturally more equanimous within our marriage.

I wasn't aware of my dependence on home until it was upended. I don't mean having a roof over my head. Everyone needs that. I missed the qualities I had imbued in the Pink House—a peacefulness that brought vitality, the invitation to be both still and creative. The walls held me. It was more than protection. It was a sanctuary. I could let go to the bone.

Gradually, over those four years of moving, the references for home that I knew only as external started to take up residence inside me. Homes historically had provided grounding and anchoring, places to relax and spread. Now, those same qualities were sourced from within—they internalized. When I paused to take a fresh look, I saw that I carried a tangible sense of something new in my center. I no longer needed to rely on the external trappings being just so.

This was a mighty good thing. It meant I could adopt a

lifestyle with greater mobility without having to micromanage my living situation. By taking home with me wherever I went, I didn't have to sweat finding the perfect home.

Thus, something cooked out of me. Something better took its place.

To understand how a seemingly interminable sense of loss could flip to something much brighter, a bit more context might be in order. One, I had wanted to downsize. To live with a smaller footprint and spend less time and energy managing stuff. Two, I had a goal to be free to travel, extensively and overseas, without the burden of managing a truckload (or shipping container) of possessions. If you add one and two together, you get an appetite for agility. To achieve it, something inside had to give.

Hello, husband. Hello, outsize remodel. Together, they gave me all the grist I needed to propel me to my dream, even if I went there kicking and screaming. My friends sang my woes right alongside me.

"You must really miss the Pink House. How much longer will the remodel take?"

"Two years? Have you tried laying out a project plan?"

"Three years? I've never heard of such a thing. How can you stand it?"

"Four years? How can that even be?"

They guessed I was being patient. I wasn't. When it became obvious there was no gaining back the original sense of stability that home held for me, I saw my choice with stark clarity. Keep trying (to no avail), or stew in the discomfort of the illusion as it cooked its way through. Knowing a thing or two about the power of deconstruction, I opted for the stew. Sitting in the fire is a bitch, but I know that once I get to the other side it's so worth it.

There are a few things I can say with certainty about how the process ended up working its way through. It wasn't fast; it took years. It wasn't a linear, step-by-step progression. I wasn't in control. However, I did what I could do, namely riding the wave of challenge and churn. Not always artfully but more often than not willingly.

The point? Well, it's not a lesson in remodeling and merging households. Rather, it's about how I gained something of true magnitude only by letting go of something I held near and dear. My previously unquestioned ideal about home eventually separated out. Once the separation occurred, I could let it fall away. In its place, a solidity they don't stock in the furniture or hardware store. The kind that moves with me, holds me from within and extends further than any walls can contain.

Part IV
Manifesting

What you seek is seeking you.

Rumi

CREATING

Olympian

Five and a half years into my career, I discovered my superpower in an unlikely place: a corporate merger. Most people dread such a thing, but where others resist change, I see possibility. Where they brace for destruction, I find creation.

From a business-model perspective, the merger made sense. Two hospital systems blending. One was comprised of large urban hospitals, the other was a network of small hospitals. It also held the promise of vertical integration—a fancy way of saying that services such as home health and ambulance were part of the deal. This merger broke the mold. There were no nauseating layoffs or reductions in force, and leadership kept communication transparent.

I learned about it three months after relocating to Minneapolis for my new job. Sarah, my boss, made it her business to set me up for success by loaning me out to the chief strategist. He was charged with building a unifying operations plan. My workload snowballed as I took on new assignments, and I ended up working evenings and weekends on tight deadlines. I loved it because I was at the table as a new design was taking shape. We were building the structure and strategy for a new enterprise.

Jim was a strategist's strategist and a mentor who gave me as much rope as I could handle. He took me under his wing during the integration phase, and when the dust settled, he became my new manager. Tall and dapper, Jim glided into meeting rooms like an Olympian in a tailored suit. He took command without anyone noticing what he'd done or how he'd done it.

When I watched him steer planning sessions for the board or executive team, I marveled. Nothing escaped him. He synthesized and drew laser-sharp distinctions while others were still digesting basic data from ten minutes earlier. He leveraged dry wit and a wry smile to tack the discussion as needed. Jim insisted on rigorous discussion with minimal contention. With his systems mind and velvet tongue, everything was clearer for the decision-makers involved. I was in awe of his craft.

In retrospect, I loved it because I was born to love it. I came into this life with the makings of a strategist. Jim's work mirrored a latent talent in me.

We differed, though, in most other ways. He was smooth, I was staunch. He was custom-made, I was off-the-rack. While he was conceiving the structure of the newly merged organization, he also was planting a master garden and training for marathons. I, on the other hand, could take on only one major challenge at a time.

It's hard to imagine the twists and turns my career might have followed had I never met Jim. He showed me how to facilitate groups. I learned by watching him. When he gave me the lead on a bold initiative to create a center of excellence with our emergency rooms and ambulance service, I learned about a unique leadership skill I carry. It's the ability to create—more so than find—common ground.

The seeds of who I was and who I could be were sprouting.

See reality.

See possibilities.

Lead groups to discover their own ideas.

Design and create.

muse

I'm sitting in my friend Gary's kitchen and watching him concoct one of his favorite breakfasts, an uber-healthy smoothie with fruit, greens and powdered products with detoxifying properties. He's a prolific music composer, commercially very successful, and I'm about to ask him the question that's been consuming me: How do you create? What I really mean is: How do you produce such works of beauty when I'm drowning in self-help trying to crack the code on creativity?

The irony, which I couldn't see then, was that I spent my days creating—memos, strategies, business plans—even as I kept searching for the key to becoming "creative." It was the early 1990s, and I'd drunk deep from the well of spiritual celebrities. A philosophy of sorts about creating and creativity had woven its way into the mainstream, and I soaked it up.

If it was so easy to create, why did I find it so hard? Money wasn't growing on trees for me, and clients weren't coming out of the woodwork. For Gary, both were happening. I figured I was missing a key step or doing something wrong. From my perch at the kitchen island, I asked him point blank, "How do you create?"

He looked at me. There was a long pause as he processed the question.

"What do you mean, how do I create?"

"Well, you're a composer. You do it for a living and on a schedule. I figured you'd be able to describe it."

"I've never really thought about it," he said. "It just comes. Why do you ask?"

"I've been thinking about creativity, and creating what I want, and I want to get better at it."

Another pause. Then, "I guess there's a flow I tune in to, and the music is just there."

Our worlds were so different, and I wanted mine to be more like what I perceived of his. Comparatively speaking, it looked juicy and spontaneous. Adventurous and bold. If only he could tell me how he did it, maybe I could import the process to my world, to make it more like an artist's world.

"But does the flow come out of nowhere? You must be doing something." In other words, give me the recipe. There's got to be one.

"I'm not doing anything. When I write jingles for ads, I meet with the agency. They brief me on the purpose, the product and the audience they want to reach."

Okay, I thought, that's the input. But I want to see how the sausage is made.

"For TV soundtracks, I watch the whole episode. A bunch of times, sometimes without sound. I'm following the emotional tone as the episode progresses. I sit at the keyboard following my senses, hearing something in my mind and moving my fingers to produce the sounds."

"What you hear—where does that come from?"

"I couldn't tell you. It's just there."

"All the time?"

"Sure." He seemed puzzled I would think otherwise.

"It doesn't come and go? You don't have a muse?"

"No, it's just there."

It sounded a bit like something that happened in my world when I was working.

"So, writing a piece of music for you is kind of like writing a memo for me? I've done it so many times, I don't have to think about how to do it."

"I don't write memos, so I couldn't say exactly, but it sounds about right."

There it hung, my partial answer, taking me only as far as a correlation you might find on an SAT exam. Memo is to jingle as businessperson is to composer.

It offered a bit of framing, but I still didn't know how the sausage—the soundtrack, even the memo—was made. His creations and his creative process seemed like magic compared to what I was doing and how I was doing it.

At least he'd cleared one thing up, a distinct contradiction to what some book authors claim: no muse needed.

try softer

Making a living in Ashland, Oregon, wasn't altogether easy, but the town was a mighty magnet for spiritual seekers with its natural beauty and laid-back charm. Home to a university, the internationally acclaimed Oregon Shakespeare Festival, and a few branches of government—that was about it for large employers. As a transplant, I heard I wouldn't be trusted right away. Fortunately, that's not how it went.

Ten miles up the highway, in Medford, the region's largest town, two hospitals and dozens of physician-owned specialty clinics thrived. When I hung out my consulting shingle, the medical professionals called. My prior experience in big healthcare systems wasn't immediately transferable to the smaller projects I led—recruiting administrators, improving process flow, succession planning—but it was close enough. The bridge I'd built from banking into healthcare now did double duty, easing the transition into professional work in a town where I knew virtually no one.

One introduction led to another. People listened, really listened, when we met over coffee or at business socials. Life moved at a pace that was different from what I'd experienced in New York and Minneapolis. No long commutes to buy supplies or get to work. With fewer everyday pressures—barring the dilemma of how to make ends meet—people in the community were present for each other. When I told my story about putting everything in storage, driving across the country looking for home and then discovering Ashland, they got it. It helped that I wasn't a California transplant.

When a person clearly wants to make a mark, has energy to burn and creative ideas, people notice. If they're clever, these people leverage that chutzpah for their vision and recruit that person to work for free. That's how Lu fished me.

Lu was a five-foot-ten redheaded pistol. Her day job was economic development, touting the advantages of relocating businesses to the valley. In her downtime, she did whatever she damn well wanted. I loved her for that. Twenty-five years older than I, Lu took me under her wing.

While decent-paying jobs were hard for anyone to find, it was especially tough for women. The solution, Lu and her associates believed, was for women to form businesses. But without savings, they'd need loans—which were impossible to get unless one didn't need them. Lu and her friends envisioned a nonprofit that would train women who wanted to start small businesses and help them gain access to credit.

It was the perfect trifecta: Women. Finance. Education. Plus, rubbing elbows with movers and shakers on a worthy cause. Of course, I told Lu, I'd be happy to donate my time. I was fine taking on unfamiliar tasks since it meant more learning. Yes, I'd serve on the founding board.

Design meetings were exhilarating. We brainstormed about the mission, board composition, programs and the volume of women we could serve. Ideas flowed freely, and decisions came easily by consensus. Thus, Southern Oregon Women's Access to Credit (SOWAC) was born.

One of the designers, Mary, also lived in Ashland and had strong community roots. Unbeknownst to me, she was interested in the director position, a paid role. She called me about it.

"I want to check in with you about the position," she said.

"Sure," I replied. "What about it?"

"I'm thinking about throwing my hat in the ring." She then explained why.

"That's great!"

"Really? Are you sure?" Apparently it wasn't what she'd expected from me.

"Of course! You'll be fantastic! Best news I've heard all week."

"Oh. I thought you might want the position."

"Me? No! I never thought of going after it. You, on the other hand, you have exactly what we need. If you get it, it will make everything work better."

She did. And it did propel the launch of SOWAC.

Leading a new organization was the furthest thing from my mind, despite what Mary and others saw in me. I didn't need or want to be the jill-of-all-trades for a start-up.

The fire in my belly had to do with how leaders lead. Specifically, models that didn't rely on command and control. Approaches that honored individuality alongside organizational needs. Nonpatriarchal approaches. The feminine side of leadership intrigued me. As Lily Tomlin quipped, "Why not try softer?"

So, I did what any experimenter might do. I created a lab to test my ideas: a circle of ten women. Lu was at the top of the list.

I handpicked the participants and named it simply Women In Leadership. They were a diverse group: a realtor, county administrator, orthodontist, minister, restaurant owner, bookkeeper, state agency director. They came to the first gathering out of intrigue. When the two hours ended, it was unanimous. They wanted more.

We set up monthly meetings that I facilitated around provocative questions. The more radical the concept, the more they leaned in. Even the most introverted, the most self-protective, came around before long, sharing stories of past and present, voicing doubts, hopes, hurts, possibilities. The others responded with compassion laced with dares to be bolder.

While each member's professional expertise barely overlapped with the others', the women found deep commonality in speaking their truth, naming their pigeonholes, taking risks, testing their confidence, and wanting another way, not knowing how to do it, and witnessing it in each other, one monthly step at a time.

The circle met for the three years I lived in Ashland. Then for another year after I relocated 250 miles north to Portland and commuted solely for these sessions. After I stepped back— the monthly commute grew difficult—they met for another thirty years and updated their name to Women Who Lunch. Their commitment to courage and truth wove a tight bond and shaped a circle that lasts to this day.

rock star

Scoring Daedalus Project tickets wasn't easy—they sold out each year—but my friend Judy had managed it. The annual fundraiser for AIDS, sponsored by the Oregon Shakespeare Festival, embodied everything Judy loved about creativity and the arts. Raucous and wild, the Shakespearean actors veered away from the Bard for this celebratory evening, staging big dance numbers and slapstick comedy—any skit, spoof or parody they wanted to perform. The evening began with a parade, during which performers showcased hats scaled to Alice in Wonderland proportions as donors bid up their value.

I was electrified, mesmerized by the originality. The concert was off the charts, grittier and more sensational than anything I'd seen on Broadway or in London's West End.

"This is aMAZing!" I shouted to Judy over the jubilant roar of the audience.

She smiled back, knowingly. This wasn't her first year as a patron.

"I can't beLIEVE it!" I continued.

Then I mused over the contrast between the performers and me, the future I might have had if I'd stuck with the piano and acted in more school plays rather than studying and competing in sports. For one revelrous instant, it seemed conceivable that I, too, could have been a member of this merry band of warriors unreservedly expressing their full selves. If only my parents had encouraged me to stay with my musical training, I thought.

I probably said as much to Judy. A moment later I was overcome with envy. From there, a series of illogical leaps.

If only my parents had made me practice. (They tried.)

If only I'd pursued a musical discipline. (I flat out didn't want to when I was a kid.)

If only I'd had the chance. (It was there, but I didn't take it.)

If only I could have been one of these people. (What does that even mean?!)

The theater buzzed until the end, and the final curtain closed after midnight. I floated home on a high. If the job of the performers had been to infect us with joie de vivre, they'd succeeded. The thrill lasted for days.

As I let the experience percolate, I admitted to myself what I wanted: my own rock-star moment. I'd sing again, train with a teacher and put on a concert. Of course, it would be a side gig, not a career change. I knew, or perhaps was conditioned to believe, I couldn't make a living in the arts. Nevertheless, I was dead serious.

My new teacher, Donna, was versatile and focused. Between weekly lessons, I practiced at home while gazing out the picture window in my living room. Cassette tapes containing warm-up drills and piano accompaniment for songs Donna wanted me to rehearse were my little workhorses. My vocal range expanded and, with time, I learned to traverse the passaggio, to smoothly move between soprano and alto. My vocalist ear sharpened; I could hear more detail in what professional artists do with timing and intonation.

Donna hosted semiannual recitals for her students. She told me I was ready before I thought I was. She rented the Barn, a small, intimate theater, and it was filled to the brim with family and friends on that Saturday evening. I sat two rows from the back with Judy, awaiting my turn. Any butterflies in my stomach were buffeted by delight in seeing each student bravely take the stage and share a piece they'd developed.

Donna and I had prearranged that she would turn over the accompaniment to my friend Gary, a professional musician, who was visiting Ashland for the weekend. He'd made the offer earlier in the day; we hadn't rehearsed.

When Donna announced I was next, I walked to the stage and Gary slid onto the bench at the grand piano. A broad smile spread across his face as he looked directly at me.

"What key?" he asked.

I told him, and his hands flexed across the keyboard

without a glance. Nor did he need the sheet music for the song I'd chosen, Carole King's "You've Got a Friend." As he rolled through the introduction, the audience exhaled, their jitters dissipating.

During the opening chord progressions, I felt something shift inside me, too. This wasn't just about music anymore—it was about the woman I was becoming, the one who had traded spreadsheets for sheet music and corporate targets for vocal scales.

When I began, both words and sound came easily. What Gary did at the keyboard perfectly complemented my voice and elevated my performance. At one point, I looked out at the crowd and saw Judy. She was smiling through her tears, liquid love flowing down her cheeks. So many connections—with the music, with Gary, with Judy, with strangers simply taking in what was passed to them in three minutes of live music—filled me in ways words can't describe.

It was a fine-enough delivery with no hiccups, and it satisfied me to the core. After that milestone, I had more confidence to press on.

For several months, I worked with Donna to build out the repertoire for a private concert. Then, with her help, I designed the program with solos and duets that she and I would do together with her at the piano. The songs would be interspersed with readings by Judy and another friend, Devorah. The last piece, "Amazing Grace," would be sung a cappella.

I reserved the Ashland Community Center, by Lithia

Park, for a one-time, one-evening performance followed by light refreshments. Then, I invited all my friends. They came.

Was it a dream come true? In every possible way, yes. Because the woman who commanded the stage was different from the woman who'd arrived in Oregon from Minnesota four years earlier. She had softened. Her will was every bit as strong, but applied in new directions.

I had stepped off the corporate ladder (not for the last time) and was making deliberate moves to create a life of my own design—a life increasingly consistent with my nature and my desires. I was learning how to function as an independent consultant while unleashing my creativity and sensuality. The drive to win, to succeed, was in the process of being supplanted by a will to feel, sense and taste life.

The seeker was becoming a finder.

white

My parents loved houses, and they bought and restored many over the years. One in particular stands out: a 150-year-old farmhouse on 80 acres in New Hampshire. It had no insulation. In winter, the accumulation of frost on the inside of the bedroom windows mirrored the snow on the outside window ledge. It needed work.

When I started shopping for my first home, my sister, who has a keen eye for bargains, assumed that was how I'd roll, too.

"Absolutely not," I told her. "I don't want a fixer-upper."

"Why not?" Elizabeth asked, surprised.

"I don't have the patience. I want a house that already feels like a home."

At the time I was living with a friend, Cate, at her house in Southeast Portland. We both knew it was temporary—I was in her spare bedroom on the heels of an abrupt and permanent exit from a ten-year romance. Cate was my safe and steady harbor as I got back on my emotional feet.

After work and on weekends, I pored over listings and frequently went to viewings with my realtor, AnnMarie. Those four months of house-hunting felt like forever, though in retrospect they were barely a flash. The challenge was that Portland was dominated by Craftsman models and I wasn't interested in stocky, boxy designs. I wanted the peaked, uplifting lines of an English cottage.

One Sunday, AnnMarie insisted I see a house in Northeast Portland that had just been listed. It was an estate sale. The prior owner was an elderly fellow, an accomplished artist. He had died in his chair in the living room.

We parked beneath one of the plum trees on the parking strip and walked up the gentle slope of the lawn. Inside, the sound of our shoes reverberated across the oak floor; the house had no furnishings. I took my first few steps into the living room and admired the marble-encased fireplace. With a 180-degree turn to the left, I faced the dining room with its three casement windows opening to the front porch. The rooms were separated by a thick archway that squeezed me through a passageway; it reminded me of an entrance to a courtyard.

That's when I knew.

"I could live here," I whispered to myself.

I'd rejected houses because of their location, their floor plan, their lighting or their general funkiness, but there was nothing about this home that made me recoil other than the exterior paint color (pink). It had two stories and a full basement for storage. All the living could easily be done on the first floor. For a 1945 house, the main bedroom and bathroom were oversized but not too big. The circular floor plan placed the bedrooms and bath in the back facing west and looking onto the garden, while the kitchen, dining room and living room faced east toward the lawn and the street. Before the estate put the house on the market, the upstairs painting studio was refinished to create a fully carpeted bonus room with five sets of windows that flooded the space with natural light and provided elevated views of the garden and treetops throughout the neighborhood. I sensed I'd be able to rest my bones and my soul here. It was an uncomplicated knowing that simply was; no big revelation or flashes of lightning. No need for a second opinion. I made an offer the next day. It was accepted two days after that.

"You bought this home all by yourself!" my mother crooned in her Southern accent, when I told her I'd found the perfect place.

"Yep," I replied. It had never occurred to me that I might acquire a house another way.

"You didn't need a man to cosign or buy it for you," she went on. "That's not the way it was in my generation. Women didn't do that. They needed men."

A few days later, the significance of what she'd said sank in. She'd never urged me to buy a house, but she was over the moon when I did. It was something outside her realm of possibility when she was my age. She genuinely felt sympathetic joy, and celebrated my achievement as much as if it had been her own.

When I arrived on my new doorstep after the closing,

keys to all the locks in hand, it was to meet the delivery driver. The driver pulled up in a small white truck and single-handedly lifted my new mattress and box spring up the front steps and into the bedroom. Aside from the bed set, the total of my belongings included nine small pieces of furniture, a car, two bikes, clothes, books, a stereo, CDs and a thirteen-inch color TV.

"Where are you?" Eric asked me on the phone. "Outside somewhere?"

He was calling from the office. He worked on my team and had called to check in about a project he was managing while I took a few hours to get settled in the new place.

"No. I'm in the living room. There's nothing in here except me and the rocking chair I'm in."

"Huh. Quite an echo."

"Yeah. I hear it, too."

Over the years that followed, I was in no rush to fill up the house. I took my time. Decorating was a leisurely, years-long process because anything I added had to meet two criteria: beauty and function. Ideally, it also was on sale. I couldn't have anticipated my little English cottage would eventually blossom into a nest, a sanctuary that embraced all who visited, whether for an evening, a weekend or an extended stay.

It's the home where I learned how to create home. Over the fourteen years I lived there, the house itself nurtured countless souls who ventured in from the cold and bristling ways of the world. The decor was simple yet not stark, and the net effect was that people could hear themselves think. They could feel their hearts beat. Everyone was held by the energy of the house, and they knew it. I eventually achieved what I set out for—to create a haven for me and all who came. Looking back, I'm struck by how naturally this sanctuary emerged. Where I often charged toward goals, here I seemed to be following something that was already trying to happen.

When I settled into a regular meditation routine, I set up a corner in my bedroom—a folded towel atop the wood floor, two throw pillows, one small blanket for cool mornings. Walking by it on the way to the bathroom would remind me to sit.

Within months, something shifted. What had started as a fifteen-minute habit had become the anchor of my day. The bedroom corner felt too small for what was happening. I moved upstairs to a nook created by a structural post, upgraded to a proper meditation cushion and added a votive candle that I lit each morning—a small ritual.

Soon I wasn't sitting alone. A community of meditators formed, and Sunday mornings found up to eight of us in a circle in the second story bonus room. The house was becoming something I hadn't envisioned—not just a sanctuary for friends and family, but a gathering place for beginner meditators who sought the same inner quiet I'd found.

That's when I converted an unfinished corner of the second floor, an attic room with narrow walls and a tiny eyebrow window, into my private alcove. This room would be mine alone. While I was at it, I'd insulate the entire upstairs.

Which brings me to color.

Once the framing, insulation, drywall, oak flooring and trim were done, it was time to choose paint. I'd used bold hues throughout the first floor of the house—a melon color in the living room, chocolate brown in the bath, apple green in the main bedroom. What I learned about meditation practice and color convinced me to put aside my personal taste for saturated hues.

Paulina reminded me that white sets a stage for so much to land on—to appear and then disappear without residual or lasting imprint. As the least imprintable color, white could serve as energetic Teflon, so less of what was released during practices would affix over time. I'd seen firsthand how meditation burns things off—beliefs, attitudes, emotional attachments—and these invisible fumes can lodge in material objects. I didn't want that.

Travels through Europe in my twenties and forties influenced my thinking as well. I had visceral experiences inside cathedrals and chapels while visiting Italy, Spain and England. In many, I felt the effect created by centuries of prayer. The spaces were stamped with angelic warmth. It was beyond the architecture, stained glass windows, statues and tapestries. Something in the air itself. As soon as I stepped outside those buildings, it was notable that I was leaving a unique atmosphere. The accumulation of these moments contributed to my growing sense of evidence that buildings retain energetic imprints. And as beautiful as those sacred spaces were, I wanted something different for my home. I wanted a palette that remained as clear and fresh as possible, whether the energy being released into the room was glorious or gloomy, elevated or depressed.

So, I went with an appealing noncolor. Mascarpone, by Benjamin Moore. It's a warm, creamy white with subtle yellow undertones. I liked it so much I used it for all three rooms—the office, my new private meditation room and the bonus room. A single color tied the whole upstairs together, subtly, undramatically.

However, it took a little shift within me to go in this direction. Like that of many Westerners, my identity was derived in part from my home. Or perhaps it was the other way around—how I decorated had to express not just my preferences but the way I thought of myself. It all added up to a particular portrayal of Kira. I confess Pottery Barn and Williams Sonoma played a role in image definition at the Pink House—the bedside tables, the curtain rods, a hanging mirror. For the times, they projected a form of success, of having arrived at a certain desirable station in life.

I had to drop it, at least enough of it. I had to resist the urge, plus the momentum, to keep declaring myself through color and decor. The years to come would teach me to appreciate neutrality and spaciousness, but I wasn't there yet. I had just enough recognition that Paulina's advice was sound: white, as a neutral, would create a space for things not of this world to come and go. After weeks of consideration, I knew this was right. The grand statement was to not make a grand statement.

It's clear to me now that the "I" who decided to drop the attachment to style found a way to favor the person I had yet to become. I was learning to create without having to shape all the bits. To allow room for more to happen than what I alone could muster. To let a calling lead me into mysteries I couldn't yet imagine, yet longed to discover.

The first time I sat in the completed meditation room, under its sharply vertexed ceiling, the far wall awash in early-morning light, I felt myself ascend with virtually no effort. I was taken up in the silence to a quiet bliss. A space that, both inwardly and outwardly, breathed possibility.

Easter

Almost three decades after saying goodbye to organized religion, I stepped back into an Episcopal church for a Sunday service. This time, I didn't go alone. I was with my fiancé, who, despite not being religious, had fond memories of a Catholic priest whose homilies inspired and encouraged him to think about life in ways he hadn't before. Our mission that Easter Sunday was to see Anne, the visiting minister and a dear friend. Though retired, she subbed for priests away from their parish. Beloved by her former congregation, she presided that day. If my fiancé was drawn to what he saw and heard, we'd ask her to officiate our wedding. He was captivated. So we did.

Anne is as smart as she is gracious, with an eye that's keenly observant of the ways of the world. Whether she's giggling or howling with laughter, her wit can cut to the quick. As a matter of practice, she never starts her day without first reading, meditating and praying. She loves her silent (and I mean silent) retreats once or more each year. Her words that Sunday were pitch perfect, holding us rapt with the power to transport.

We lived in different towns and didn't see each other often, but she'd shared copies of her sermons on various topics over the years. Our conversations always spelunked into deep spiritual waters, territory where experience could defy words. Her remarkable facility with language turned our joint explorations into a glide, not a slog, toward clarity.

While her sermon that misty Sunday morning was brilliant, something else had me spellbound. As she performed the Eucharist, I peered into aspects of the ritual I'd never noticed before. In the Episcopal Church, as in many Christian traditions, the Eucharist stands as the heart of worship. Also called Holy Communion, it's a sacred ritual performed every Sunday, transforming ordinary bread and wine into holy elements through ancient prayers. For many, it's not just symbolic—it's a mysterious encounter with the divine, a moment where heaven and earth meet. While the ritual follows a prescribed form passed down through centuries of church tradition, each priest brings their own presence to this sacred dance.

Watching Anne at the altar was like nothing I'd ever witnessed at the Episcopal church of my youth. She invoked the forces of her tradition, and the forces responded. She stood before the altar and faced the congregation. Her stature silently shifted in keeping with the purpose. She appeared slightly elevated, stately. As if on a deep in-breath, her physical presence expanded. Preparing the wine and bread for consecration, she entered a fullness of silence. It appeared that thoughts of worldly matters were swept from her mind.

Her eyes grew radiant and a smile crossed her face in response to something only she saw. Her expression shone with joy. Before any words were spoken, she was transposed into another realm. Then, when she spoke, it was as if her lungs were releasing air infused and powered by something invisible. Her awareness was both inward and outward, feeling and acting, turning up and shining forth.

While she glowed, I became aware of what was hovering beneath the church roof for all of us. The presence of divine love. We were no longer just humans in pews. We were visited by a presence. It pressed into us with its warmth and caring. If offered a quiet form of creative inspiration. It reflected the connected web of all things. It provided a glimpse of the divine intersecting with humanity.

In the tradition of the Episcopal Church, wafers and wine are a physical representation of the body and blood of Christ. But it was through Anne, as an instrument, that we witnessed genuine exultation. Seeing it spread across her face, in her smile, in the way she tipped her head back and looked aloft, somehow opened the door for us to be touched, too. Her visible experience of connection to something holy—her receptivity and engagement with it—provided a footpath to walk along. I found myself naturally turning up, opening, receiving from a higher order.

It didn't matter what that giving presence was called. Names weren't important. What mattered was this precious moment of intentional celebration, where we were lifted out of the humdrum of our day-to-day lives into a refined position among the forces behind this living tradition. Because we were privy to her jubilation, we caught a whiff of our own. Public, yet intimate. Personal, yet shared.

What a gift, actually. For her. Through her. To her congregants. The ritual provided a means to move into a state of being that was vast and infused with the magnificence of spirit.

If that's what transpired at the church of my upbringing, I missed it. I don't remember it that way. There were motions and people went through them. It felt heavy, dire, in contrast to this lightness and natural elevation. The men of the church were so serious and without a visible shred of joy when they took to the altar. Anne, on the other hand, was truly in communion, each movement growing out of her experience, each expression reflecting how touched she was to be in that very moment.

When the service ended, I asked my fiancé what he thought. He looked straight ahead and let out a long exhale. Then a gentle smile. "I'm reminded of the priest I liked so much in Colorado. Father Marty's homilies were the primary reason I attended St. Stephen's."

Anne created. It wasn't art or music. She created experiences that were otherwise elusive. A liminal interface between the divine and the human. Her sermons and Eucharists transported people deep inside themselves, and then transcendently beyond. She was able to connect us to qualities many of us yearned for. She did it in a way unique unto her. Underneath it all was her deeply personal desire to follow the leading of the spirit. And as she did, in sharing it with us, we could, too.

grope

Twyla Tharp would never label herself a sage. She knows herself as a bold choreographer. Starting in the seventies, she wowed audiences with her avant-garde modern-dance performances. More recently, hordes have fallen in love with her exquisite writing. She knows how to make peace with the discomfort of the unknown; she wades, over and over, into unchartered creative waters and returns with new moves. Then she shows us how we can do our version of the same. Inspired by *The Creative Habit*, I decided to write a creative autobiography —a short personal sketch meant to help surface my own creative roots.

My earliest creations came through my hands—knitting, croqueting, sewing and baking. Doing it right was important. Doing it right meant I was right. Every slip-up was excruciating. Rip out a seam after stitching fabric on the wrong sides. Dump a whole bowl of ingredients because I mismeasured. Sure, I'd do what I could to salvage the situation. Usually, it worked out just fine. All I lost was time. But inside, the halo of hoped-for perfection fell off. The finished product now had a built-in mistake, and if it wasn't perfect, it was marred. It didn't matter that no one would ever know or notice, or care if they did notice. If it wasn't right per the instruction, it said something to me about me. Its flaw was my flaw. Every mistake ground at me. Following directions to a tee was my insurance—my chosen method of defense against an unconscious concept that deep down I wasn't good enough.

It wasn't just my interpretation about outcomes that was mangled. I had grown dependent on printed directions. I wasn't interested in improvising. Someone somewhere had to know what they were doing, or the steps wouldn't have been written down. Following them was my best bet for a successful creation.

I was no Twyla Tharp. Not then. Not ever.

While I have neither her skill nor her technique, I eventually veered from my fixed, only-one-way-to-do-it-right approach. I turned in a new direction on purpose. There was no intention to change. It just emerged. One day I realized: Hey, that's what I do. It came to light through darkness. It's been evolving ever since. I call it groping.

My husband likes and needs his sleep. Often he doesn't get enough. Daylight peeking through windows, a commuter car barreling down the street, or his mind all abuzz will send him upright before he gets seven hours. To maximize the likelihood of deep sleep—whether night or day—we installed blackout curtains that supplement the blinds. The idea is to block all light short of nailing plywood to the window frame. The curtains work well; I can't see anything when I get out of bed on winter mornings. Not even a faint shadow. I leave the light off in hopes my husband won't notice my movements. With my arms extended in front of me, I patter toward the bedroom door. Nine times out of ten my fingers land to the left of the doorframe, and from there I run my hands along the wall. Eventually I round the small corner and come to the door. I feel my way.

When it comes right down to it, I'm a groper. Not in the aberrant grab-her-breasts sort of way. It's about activating senses, awakening awareness, to eventually register what's actually there. I probe to explore in the midst of uncertainty and when things are unfamiliar. If I have zero idea what's ahead, I put out feelers. That's how I gather useful references. The sensation is quite tactile—even when I'm not physically touching anything.

In the bedroom, the wall exists and I know it's there, but it's almost never where my foggy morning brain thinks it is. No supposition will move the wall to where I imagine it. As I tiptoe, what I'm after is the real thing. A click with reality. A click I can count on because it's real. My eyes being of no use, I revert to my fingertips. My bearings come from groping.

It's not altogether different for me in meditation. Twists and turns are frequent, as in this recent meditation:

I sit, cross-legged, on my meditation pillow. I wrap a blanket around me.

My eyes close. I adjust my posture so my head rests above my hips.

My thoughts slow down. Then there's a notable pause.

What now? Where is this heading? I sometimes feel an urge to get ahead of myself.

A suspended moment. Just wait, nothing to do.

The thing that comes online next isn't the same as what came online yesterday. It's both refreshing and frustrating that I can't assign patterns. Frustrating because I prefer knowing where I'm going. Refreshing because it's liberating to surrender to what wants to happen rather than hold on to what my mind manufactures as the right thing to happen.

There's darkness. It's not black, more like deep purple.

As dark as it is, there's a sense of light within it. It's neither beaming nor flooding. Diffuse, misty yet without moisture in the earthly sense. Pervasive, permeating. Yesterday there was light, too. It was more golden, like the sun. This time it's a purer white. Interesting! Light isn't just light.

My simply becoming aware of this light brings about subtle change to the light. It grows in depth. I simply attune to its changing expression.

This unfussy attunement leads to another shift. While I start out watching as an observer, at some point I'm no longer watching from outside. I'm inside whatever I'm looking at. How'd that happen? Faster than an instant. Here one moment, there the next.

The feelers I used before don't work now. So, I drop them. As I get help from elsewhere, it's easy to lay old references down.

This space is more refined, and I suspend any attempt to define it.

From here, I need to let it show me the way. It's as though I must let a groping pair of hands be placed on whatever it wants me to notice.

Be teachable. Be navigated.

Don't argue with the vagueness or lack of familiarity.

Steady. Patient. No forcing. If I start to presume, let that go, too.

The instruction in the what and how lies inside the energetic space itself. Within the moment. I'm along for the ride, but not passively. It's a doing without doing.

My groping function gets an update, an upgrade, to match whatever is unfolding. Not unlike changing tracks on a railroad. I'm not on the local anymore. I'm on the express. It goes faster. It's more direct. The equipment isn't so very different, but the wiring allows it to operate in a way that's qualitatively different.

From here, as the tracks come and go, it's the subtle attunement of nonphysical senses that keeps me in its flow.

And on it goes.

It's not improv. It's not problem-solving or fixing. It's definitely not steering a ship in the direction I think it should go. Rather, it's being navigated. The reality I tune in to isn't just what's already present—it's the reality of what's pregnant, what's possible, the earliest indicators of a something being ushered in. The content itself can never be predicted.

I'm swept up in the choreography of the spheres. Movement can accelerate, slow, or come to a standing stillness that lasts a good long while. I can be taken up, out, or in—sometimes all three seemingly at the same time. Groping is awareness of what's there, not what I suppose is there.

It simply doesn't work if I go looking for what I think should be there. I have to relax, loosen, let go, become transparent to whatever presents itself in order to catch it. It's not this, it's not that, drop the comparisons . . . Ah, here, now it's real. I sense what's landed. Only then can I rest on it.

The meditation experience is fresh and new each time, even though the pathway is repeated—just as the journey to find the bedroom door is new every morning despite the wall never moving. I often pass markers I've seen before. But if the actual experience, inside the meditation, were identical day after day, I would either be in a rut or at a plateau. Pressing boundaries is what builds my spiritual muscle. Every time I cross a threshold, I'm in new territory.

Here's a new mystery.

How am I going to find my way around?

Grope.

I used to get frustrated when the terrain changed. I would get the hang of things in a new space, earn my bearings, gain confidence that I could find my way around. Then it would shift. Different qualities. Some vaguely familiar markers and others I could barely make out. Since it's in my nature to want to get things right, I found it hugely frustrating. Here I go, starting all over again. Deciphering. Trying to fathom what's before me. No words. A vague sense of qualities. Sometimes I felt so duped it was all I could do to slow down and simply be with whatever was there, including my own befuddlement.

Feeling lost didn't mean anything was wrong. It just meant I didn't recognize where I was, and didn't yet have the faculties to tune in to what was actually there.

I've come to see that groping serves a double purpose: to feel my way, and to broaden the very capacity to feel my way. I'm a better decoder the more I decode.

With time, my relationship to these ever-broadening horizons has evolved. It's more exciting, more fun, to wander into new places and spaces. It's also exciting to peel back a layer on a space I'm familiar with and see something more of its essence.

Slowly. Patiently. Feeling my way from a bearingless position. Engaging without controlling. Being with waiting as details and nuances gradually come into view.

As for the method of groping itself, there are many sensory modes I instinctively engage. In the physical world, groping happens largely through touch and feel. In the spiritual realms, it's still sensory, just not with bodily hands. For work projects, it happens through a blend of intellect and vision.

I've learned that the art, in all these arenas, is to grope without grasping. Activate my curiosity without demanding.

Notice without grabbing. Groping is simply my effort to find and comprehend. It's a means of exploration that, at its best, doesn't predefine or presuppose.

It requires a standpoint beyond fixity. Resting, to start, in the unknown, with neither the old references nor the old bearings. (Perhaps a parallel to Twyla after all.) That's where it begins. But it doesn't end there.

This discovery didn't happen overnight. I spent decades learning to follow directions perfectly, only to discover a greater skill in navigating without them. As for the sense that there's something wrong with me, that started dissipating with meditation, which opened doors to a clearer vision of what's real and what's not. The study of structural thinking and structural consulting drove it home. Concepts about myself can feel as real as the fact that the sky is blue, without being true at all. Such beliefs still creep into my creating process, but more infrequently. And I can admire the result even when I know mistakes were made along the way.

Groping is an organic process. I use it in my career as much as I do in everyday life. But because it's internal, it's not obvious to an onlooker what I'm doing.

After a recent consulting engagement, members of the leadership team were stunned. They said our work together was unlike any strategy session they'd taken part in before. They were surprised by the absence of tedium. Their path forward felt more like inspiration than work. My approach, which lives outside any formula, catapulted them beyond what they thought possible, and with far less anxiety about change. I enjoy the way mysteries unfold when I cocreate with clients. Plus it pays the bills and affords me a way to offer value to people who are bringing good things to life.

Twyla collects ideas; I accumulate pictures of what's happening at my clients' organizations. Twyla is an inventor; I am a seer and catalyst for my clients' creations. Twyla constructs; I help deconstruct what no longer serves. Twyla imagines; I grope.

ASPIRING

the agenda

"**H**OW MANY IDEAS will people bring tomorrow?" I ask, glancing over my computer at my client. Around the table sit a city commissioner, a bureau director, a deputy director, a chief of staff and a senior policy adviser. We're finalizing tomorrow's agenda—an expensive gathering of thirty high-ranking staff from multiple bureaus.

"My bureau alone listed over sixty," says the director.

"So, all told, we're looking at more than a hundred recommendations," I say, mostly to myself.

Pause.

"Well, yeahhhhh."

I know thirty people can't possibly prioritize a hundred unvetted ideas in under two hours—not in any meaningful way, and not without justified grousing. The agenda I drafted two days ago goes out the window.

Good facilitators don't get flummoxed by direction changes. It happens all the time. We are elicitors, leading the way on a path of discovery. Discovery itself is the job of the participants. The art lies in designing a process that moves people forward, toward results, when no one can possibly know the answers ahead of time.

Of the thousands of meetings I've led, the government-sponsored ones stand out as the biggest free-for-alls. Ironic, given the rigidity of bureaucracies. Then again, if there's an outsider facilitating, perhaps people take it as permission to rattle the cage.

I usually say no to government projects. I nearly declined this one, but then said yes for two reasons: it's a short gig—helping launch a task force whose work will continue without me—and I'm intrigued by its purpose. I believe I can get them to solid ground. If motivated, they'll incline toward innovation. If complacent, they'll drag their feet, and the task force will be defunct within months. Above all, they need to see that change is possible, and they're the ones to lead it.

A tall order.

The agenda that just died is for the second of our three meetings. I know where I need to get them, but the path I had in mind is no longer viable.

"Okay," I say. "Coming out of this meeting, Commissioner, what does success look like?"

"Everyone would buy into the severity of the problem we're here to solve." He's done continuous-improvement work before, so he knows that to get groups moving in the same direction, people need to believe in a vision or agree that a problem warrants fixing.

"That's realistic," I say. "We can take time at the opening for leaders to lay out their top priorities. No breakout rooms. Everyone needs to hear them at the same time." Agreed.

"But people will doze off if one person speaks too long. Let's do it round-robin style." Agreed.

"Then, we'll peel folks off into breakout rooms to get everyone engaged. We'll give them an assignment. That way, they'll mingle while learning more about each other's challenges." Agreed.

"And let's anchor the homework this time. Instead of a blanket assignment, we'll have them codesign the specifics of the homework." Agreed.

We design a new agenda in under thirty minutes. An hour later, I hit send on the final version. It's really good.

As I walk down the hall for a glass of water, it's not the agenda itself I'm thinking about, nor the speed with which it came together. Our prep meeting could have turned to low-grade panic. It didn't. And while I tend to have a calming influence, the bigger deal is that I attuned to a flow of intelligence beyond the limits of my mind. When I operated from there, everything was smooth. Easy. No grasping. The new approach was obvious and effortlessly completed. The agenda rearranged itself, along with the outline of the final meeting.

This signaled a new milestone for me—a vivid illustration

of how my professional work converges with my ability to draw from higher realms. I didn't force a new agenda using a well-developed muscle. Instead, I gained access to a non-muscle type of strength. By actively following the line of possibility that opened for us, all I had to do was share what I saw and watch the pieces cascade into place. The end product—a workable agenda for this expensive meeting—was crisp, elegant, refined. It was embedded with clarity and not a hint of weightiness.

I knew exactly from whence the agenda emerged. As much as I value a handmade life, many of my best creations come when I cede control and function from another plane.

bells and whispers

The bells rang through my Portland home, their sound vibrating against the walls as Paulina moved methodically through the space. The ceremony began in the dining room, where she had transformed the glass-top table into an altar with colorful fabric, vibrant flower heads and a candlelit centerpiece. Together, we progressed through the house. Each room received a small plate of fresh-cut flowers encircling a tealight candle. These were offerings. Before we went on to the next room, Paulina silently lit the flame in the center of the plate, and swished a few drops of holy water onto the flowers.

"What do you most want?" she'd asked me days before this space-clearing ceremony.

She'd asked me this question before. In the fourteen years I'd lived in the house, Paulina space-cleared four times. The question always invited me to look deeper. Before the first clearing, I knew I wanted a new job. Three days later, I was given an out-of-the-box work assignment. With each successive space clearing, my desire moved further out on a continuum, shifting from the material to the sublime. Though the word Paulina used was "want," the real opportunity was for the stirrings within my heart to span the divide between heaven and earth. This is not a job my brain can carry out.

"I want a vaster experience of opening," I said, the words emerging not from calculation but from somewhere quieter within. "From the center of my heart and my whole being. To let my shields down and meet life without all the protections I've assembled."

What I was describing wasn't exactly a want. It fit a different category: aspiration. These two slants—want and aspiration—have been shaping my life since before I understood there was a difference between them.

In my early twenties, I knew exactly what wanting felt like. On the eve of college graduation, a friend wrote to me: *I have miles of confidence in you. In fifteen years, you'll either be president of the US, Mobil Oil, or the US Olympic Committee.*

He recognized my determined nature. When I wanted something, I applied myself relentlessly, and things often came together. That was my operating system: set sights, drive forward, achieve. My career became the perfect vehicle for this energy—I was hell-bent on supporting myself as an independent woman, channeling my intense nature into making things happen in the world.

In my midtwenties, I wanted to get better at squash, a game I truly loved. I improved. Out of the blue, however, I was sidelined with a knee injury no doctor could explain. During that off-court season, I wanted something new, though I couldn't yet name what it was. The impulse quietly took up residence in my heart. I returned a different player, my attention solely on the hard black ball—its movement through time and space, its angles and speed. I was the ball, feeling it, connecting with the archetype of the game without having concretely learned anything new. I started winning against players I'd never beaten. It didn't come from a worldly goal. In retrospect, I recognize it as aspiration that opened the door to a transcendent experience of the game.

In my thirties, I diligently applied visualization methods, confident they would manifest my desires. When they didn't materialize, I assumed I was doing something wrong. It was hugely frustrating because the approach I tried seemed so sensible, so obvious. Why wasn't this technique, as an add-on to my drive and proven ability to get results, turning my proverbial rags to material riches?

In my forties, I stepped off the corporate ladder and returned to independent consulting. Though I could feel what I was after—working with smart, high-integrity people whose ideas could contribute value to the world—this feeling didn't lend itself to an actionable business plan. I had to hold the unresolved tension of what I felt possible. I wanted to make a living, but my aspiration was about something beyond money.

Through trial, error and experience, I've arrived at the conclusion that some yearnings are better left wordless, while others bear fruit when defined. And I recognize that both aspirations and wantings have been alive in me all along. Occasionally, they are one and the same. But the more I respect the difference between them, the more honest I can be with myself about my motivation. And by extension, the more likely they are to come into being.

Aspiration is the one I usually hold wordlessly. In fact, the less specific, the better. I've come to understand it as a turning upward in an attitude of active receptivity. If it's too defined, it puts a limit on what's possible—both the means and the ends. My experience is that aspiration, held over time, forms a receptacle through which high spiritual beings offer help. Holding aspiration happens with spiritual muscle, not mental muscle.

Wantings are more mundane—keeping the house tidy, bingeing a TV series, going to an art gallery with a friend. I keep an eye out for the screaming desires that implore urgency. The more the tug, the more I suspect that they originate from within. Buy that maxi navy wool coat (that I don't need and have no room for in my closet). Get tickets for that concert (even though I hate crowds). Wouldn't it be handy if popular memes came with a warning? Caution: false note ahead.

The inner signals I try not to ignore are those that arrive sotto voce. In a hushed voice. These register on a sensory level—a feeling, a broad knowing—and rarely involve material things.

Instead: the inspiration to extract myself from US norms for a spell and spend winter as a digital nomad in Southern Spain—and, years earlier, the message to be with my father at the end of his life.

With practice, I've gotten better at detecting when the source is somewhere central to my being. What helps me assess its authenticity is to consider whether I'd want it even if no one else did, even if the option was never paraded before me, even if attainment eluded me my entire life.

Progress toward my aspirations is usually gradual. I have to hold them for a good long while. I don't think it's because no one's answering on the other end of the line. Rather, something in me needs to be readied to receive all that's going to be available. Sometimes, I'm actually inching forward in real, tangible ways without recognizing it's happening.

One day, I had an epiphany. What I aspired to and what spiritual forces wanted for me were aligning. Something was being dreamed for me, and I was catching the dream. It was remarkably tangible.

Not just serving my clients, but caring in a way best described as love.

Meeting mentors, masters of their craft, giants in their own right, who teach me.

Deconstructing the crystalized, crunchy parts of my personality that, left unchecked, would impede me from opening to bigger, vaster states of being.

And it was a milestone day when I realized that my desires—both aspirations and wantings—no longer have anything to do with proving myself. The new direction was toward surrender, willingly. To let go more, so the gods could work their transformational miracles. Without my list of goals. Without a vision board.

I was learning to receive inspiration and qualities of experience I never would have fathomed or asked for because until I experienced them, they were beyond my realm of understanding. They came into view, revealing their existence, because I was learning to suspend my more-narrow perception.

The deeper wisdom I've found is this: Aspiration opens the door for grace to enter. Not as a guarantee, but as a possibility. It's a grace I don't order but recognize and appreciate when it arrives. It's a virtuous cycle of aspiration, surrender and gratitude.

The worldly wants still have their place—career achievements, a beautiful home, creative projects. I pursue these with focused intention and practical effort. But alongside them runs this other current. Aspiration. Turning upward with open hands rather than grasping; creating space for grace to enter in its own time and way. It's a practice I'm still refining, this art of knowing when to drive forward and when to simply turn my face to the light, open and receive.

the list

When packing for a trip, I always reach for the basics—clothes, toiletries, medications. After that, the items are specific to my destination. Some trips call for a sun hat and a bathing suit. Others necessitate a computer.

Since I've got good spatial perception, I can pack a lot into a small carry-on. It may get heavy but it fits in the overhead bin of an airplane, and I usually use all the items I take and don't miss much of anything. It's about bundling what I need and nothing more.

The essential life-navigation kit I've assembled through years of experimentation costs next to nothing. It really is a case of the best things in life being free if you have a library card. Any item on its own can work charms—to calm, restore, inspire. Applied in unison, the items serve as a wellspring.

Whenever I forget for too long to use every part of the kit, I slip out of balance. Something's off. Once I notice I'm wobbling, I instinctively do a quick scan to pinpoint what I've been missing. Since I have evidence—direct experience—that each serves me well, there's no talking myself into doing them. I pick up where I left off and keep going.

Here are the ten things I depend on.

Meditation, to cultivate stillness and vision. I'm choosy about meditation pillows and swap them out infrequently. The same goes for the blanket I wrap around myself for sitting in cooler months. It started as a daily practice; it still is. It grew to semiannual retreats that deepen my experience and expand access to more and more dimensions of consciousness. The big booster—the icing and the cherry on top—turned out to be weekly classes at my meditation school's urban center.

Solitude, to attune. On the introvert–extrovert continuum, I land squarely in the middle. I got more than enough solitude when I lived alone. Being partnered takes a little more strategy; I'm fortunate my husband and I are well-matched when it comes to needing time to ourselves.

Aspiration, broadly and wordlessly sensed. There's no formula involved; I think that would diminish the pleasure and the possibilities. When I don't insist on the details of what I long for, the surprises that result can be quite pleasing.

Nature, amply, in its most pristine forms. My physical body, etheric body, mind and spirit experience life differently from a mountain peak, the seaside, or a tall-growth forest. Fresh air at all times is a must. Hence, my best vacations aren't city destinations. They involve reveling in natural beauty, ideally from the seat of a bicycle.

A journal, to capture inspiration, ideas, frustrations and progress. Simple college-ruled spiral notebooks are my go-to. I don't write every day, just when I need to capture an impulse that I think has staying power, or to get something onto the page so it stops rattling around inside.

Books, to draw knowledge and insight from great thinkers and sages. Truly brilliant prose and literature penetrates—my mind, my heart—in ways nothing else can. Reading is one of the best ways I've found to get over my self-musings and remind myself there's a great big world out there with people and places and happenings beyond my narrow frame. Others' realities reshape my sense of the true nature of the world around me.

Aerobic exercise, yoga, and overall body care. I was raised on tennis courts, in swimming pools and on playing fields, so I love to exercise. I came to yoga in midlife and fell in love with it—nothing else circulates the deep centers of my energy as well. I'm a clean water snob. And I prefer my fruit and veggies organic.

Caring relationships. They take all forms. People keep evolving and so does the nature of connections. I'm fortunate to have many friendships that pick right up where they left off, and to have bonds that were broken only to be repaired later.

I'm constantly reminded that purely transactional exchanges leave a lot on the table.

Creating, to respond to the force of life that propels us as humans. Whether substantial or simple, whether the outcome matches the original intent, the act of creating can teach and delight me. And frustrate me en route, too.

Opening. Always, opening. Perhaps the most important of all. This is my edge. I adopted certain constrictions at a young age, and they've proven resistant to unwinding. As the saying goes, we're all works in progress, and this is part of my ongoing work—though the word "work" doesn't match the effort. It's relaxing, loosening, moving toward vulnerability instead of away from it. Never the same path through.

Looking at this list, I smile at its simplicity. Yet reaching this point was anything but simple. Each item represents layers of experience—practices embraced and abandoned, rediscovered, and reimagined. What began as rigid disciplines softened into gentle rhythms. What I once thought were answers revealed themselves as doorways to deeper questions. My navigation kit emerged not through accumulation, but through a gradual stripping away of what wasn't essential.

A lot has changed since high school and college days, when I was unconvinced of the existence of god and carried the silent aspiration to know, not believe, the truth of the matter.

A series of experiences led me to see for myself that something big and benevolent and nonhuman was, in fact, involved.

The focus of what I want out of life has undergone a noticeable shift. I am influenced less and less by cultural norms and more by stirrings from deep within. These desires announce themselves softly, quietly. They simply are. I have a healthy confidence in my ability to bring into existence the things about which I care most, including a community of people I love and who love me. I appreciate profound connections among friends with whom I share meditation studies and practices.

Perhaps most important of all, however, is my growing sense of vision. I'm prone to paying attention to what can be seen and felt all around me. Knowing through observation. Peering into what normally goes unseen, rather than adopting new-age or age-old beliefs, or putting stock in the opinions of people smarter than I.

My way, as it turns out, is deeply spiritual and silently devotional. It does not rest on the foundation of a church or religion.

It's a solo journey sprinkled and infused with the love and influence and help of people I've already met, and many more to come.

There is still so much I don't know about the mysteries of the divine. However, once I found a path that matched my nature and my constitution, my experiences of the worlds above and below changed. The doors unfastened and I went through.

The key to it all was a practice so simple and innocuous: a consistent daily meditation. That is what flung open the doors and became the surprising linchpin of learning—about myself, the world we live in and the realms beyond.

POSTSCRIPT

WHEN I STARTED writing this memoir, it wasn't all stories. It was chock-full of conclusions I'd drawn and teachings I'd received about spirituality and life in general. A close friend read the early manuscript and reflected how preachy it was. I thought to myself: Really? Isn't everything I've written self-evident?

Well, no. I had to wrestle with myself on that one. What I thought was sharing a good thing was actually prescribing a belief system. It was self-help disguised as a memoir. Ouch.

Going back to the drawing board was good for the book and for me. I left huge swaths of writing on the cutting-room floor, and concentrated on moments when something of me was being shaped or rearranged.

Another friend read a later version and summed up her take. "Basically, this is a letter to your younger self." Indeed. The girl who didn't know if she'd ever answer the god question to her satisfaction. The young adult embarking on a career. The spiritual seeker who knew there was more to life on earth than what met the eye. The one who didn't know how it would all turn out and hadn't yet learned what navigating a life might look like.

Eventually, the seeker became the finder. Not in every

regard or about everything. But it wasn't all quest without discovery. The tipping point, for me, came through meditation. I feel incredibly fortunate to have found much of what I sought, and still seek. In saying that, I'm aware I'll never exhaust what's there to discover. The cosmos I've glimpsed is beyond my full comprehension, save awareness of certain principles and inner workings. That it's not entirely fathomable makes it all the more enticing, and to me, a beautifully worthy frontier. I don't want to stop groping, sourcing, making my way toward understanding. To me, it's more interesting than most anything else.

I recall a saying attributed to Werner Erhard. It was something like, "I look back at myself two years ago and wonder how anyone so stupid could have lived." While it's a funny thing to say, it's also profound. To me, it suggests that we can change in major and wonderful ways. For a long time, I shared that sentiment, with its focus on the past. Now, I look forward to the person I'll be two years hence.

It's likely that my toolkit will shift as I do. It will evolve and refine. I can't know today what will be needed tomorrow. But I can reliably count on my ability to discern—eventually if not immediately—adapt and keep moving onward.

SOURCES AND INFLUENCES

Sources

The following quotations and references appear in the text. Source information reflects standard scholarly editions or widely accepted modern translations.

Epigraphs
Part I

"What is this mind of mine? Where is the truth in it?"

From Farid ud-Din Attar's Mantiq al-Tayr (The Conference of the Birds), twelfth century.

Part II

"There is a voice that doesn't use words. Listen."

Widely attributed to Jalāl al-Dīn Rumi; no confirmed Persian original appears in scholarly editions.

Part III

"The wound is the place where the light enters you."

From Jalāl al-Dīn Rumi's *Masnavi-ye Ma'navi*, Book III (line ≈ 1120).

Part IV

"What you seek is seeking you."

From Jalāl al-Dīn Rumi's *Masnavi-ye Ma'navi*, Book III (line ≈ 1440).

harmony
Finley, James. "Thomas Merton: Session 1." *Turning to the Mystics*, Season 1: Center for Action and Contemplation, 2020. Podcast audio.

moan
Branch, John. "Tom Brady's Body Coach Says He Can Fix Any Injury." *The New York Times*, November 13, 2015.

names
Zimmer, Heinrich. *Philosophies of India*. Edited by Joseph Campbell. Princeton University Press, 1951.

stowaway
"Evert: Ice Maiden of Tennis." *The New York Times*, June 7, 1975.

gone then gone
Samuel Sagan. *Death, The Great Journey*. Point Horizon Institute, 2011.

try softer
Tomlin, Lily. *Lily Tomlin Live!* HBO, 1977.

Influences

The following books, ideas and other resources influenced my journey and may be of interest to readers exploring similar paths.

Spiritual Practice & Meditation

Chödrön, Pema. *When Things Fall Apart: Heart Advice for Difficult Times*

Sagan, Samuel. *Awakening the Third Eye*

Creativity & Life Design

Fritz, Robert. *Creating: A Practical Guide to the Creative Process*

Fritz, Robert. *Identity: Why It Doesn't Matter What You Think About Yourself*

Fritz, Robert. *The Path of Least Resistance: Principles for Creating What You Want to Create*

Fritz, Robert. *The Path of Least Resistance for Artists: The Structure and Spirit of the Creative Process*

Fritz, Robert. *Your Life As Art*

Tharp, Twyla. *The Creative Habit: Learn It and Use It for Life*

Organizational Leadership

Fritz, Robert. *The Managerial Moment of Truth: The Essential Step in Helping People Improve Performance*

Fritz, Robert. *The Path of Least Resistance for Managers (Revised and Expanded, 2011)*

Grenny, Joseph; Patterson, Kerry; McMillan, Ron; Switzler, Al, and; Gregory, Emily. *Crucial Conversations: Tools for Talking When Stakes Are High*

Kahane, Adam. *Collaborating with the Enemy: How to Work with People You Don't Agree with or Like or Trust*

Kegan, Robert, and Laskow Lahey, Lisa. *Immunity to Change: How to Overcome It and Unlock the Potential in Yourself and Your Organization*

Space & Environment
Kingston, Karen. *Clear Your Clutter with Feng Shui: Free Yourself from Physical, Mental, Emotional and Spiritual Clutter Forever (Revised and Updated)*

Kingston, Karen. *Space Clearing, Volume 1: The Art of Clearing and Revitalizing Energies in Buildings*

Kingston, Karen. *Space Clearing, Volume 2: How Space Clearing Works*

Kondo, Marie. *The Life-Changing Magic of Tidying Up: The Japanese Art of Decluttering and Organizing*

Death & Dying
Gawande, Atul. *Being Mortal: Medicine and What Matters in the End*

Halifax, Joan. *Being with Dying: Cultivating Compassion and Fearlessness in the Presence of Death*

Kalanithi, Paul. *When Breath Becomes Air*

Sagan, Samuel. *Death: The Great Journey* (audio, with text)

Online Resources
Autonomy and Life — www.autonomyandlife.com

Creating Your Life — www.creatortools.net

DISCUSSION GUIDE

As mentioned in the first pages of the book, I think we would all do well to open to each other and find ways to talk about the divine. Ideally, the focus of these discussions would be on direct experiences, not what we've read or what someone else has told us.

To that end, here are some questions to prompt personal reflection, group discussion and shared exploration.

ABOUT YOUR LIFE

Is the divine something you experience directly, or something you relate to through faith? Have you had moments where you felt you came in contact with something bigger than you?

How would you describe your relationship to the divine? Is there something you want—in or from that relationship—that you don't currently have?

Have major losses in your life produced major openings and realizations? Have they changed you in some way?

Sacred and secular life can be viewed as distinct and possibly opposite, or as being along a continuum. What's your viewpoint?

Healing and transformation can feel vulnerable. To what extent do you notice you're willing to open to the discomfort when the moment strikes?

What would you tell your younger self about the world, and how to approach the life ahead?

What are the burning questions about life that simmer inside you? How do you hold them, and pursue them?

If you suspend the idea that your life has a purpose and you need to find it, would that free you to live in accordance with a different principle?

What are navigational tools? What are yours? Are there new tools you've recently cultivated, or want to cultivate?

If you were to pen your spiritual memoir, what events would you include? What would the title be?

Are there concepts you held about yourself, your family and the world at large that were debunked as you gained a clearer view of reality?

ABOUT THE BOOK

What chapters were the most impactful for you? How did they speak to you?

The author uses each chapter to share an experience but avoids being prescriptive. Did you expect or want more advice? If so, about what?

In many ways, *Winnowing* is about cultivating navigational senses. How does the author's ability to navigate her spiritual journey evolve?

The author recounts several instances of loss. How did they change her?

ACKNOWLEDGMENTS

We rest on others, indeed—a principle embodied in this book's creation. I received help from countless others, starting with the earliest readers whose feedback on initial vignettes cast me in a better direction than my original concept would have taken me. Janet Tapper and David Ross encouraged story expansion. Sierra Faith delivered an essential, graceful blow by pointing out the power of first-person narrative in contrast to third-person prescriptions. Danielle Heckmeck spied the inconsistencies and gaps, and Theresa Montoya introduced a method to help each story move from here to there.

As the structure of short, distinct chapters came together, so did the idea of a serial release, which drew heaps of helpful feedback and encouragement from dozens of readers, notably Talie Harris, Jeanette Nilstein, Jan Barton, Sky O'Callahan, Dan Jamison, Wilson Silva, Rossi, Steve Spindler, Dixie Samuels, Eloise Damrosch, Areanna Lloyd, Lois Langlois, Sam Fuqua, Kelcy Benedict, Lori Eberly, Pat Burk, BethAnne Flynn, Leslie Copland, Josh Gould, Rodney Place, Kathleen McCleary, Pam Callahan, John Nieto, Valerie Bressman and Rosemary Schwimmer.

My creativity (in all endeavors) is uniquely nourished by friends and colleagues who themselves defy drift, including Judy Dolmatch, Lesley-Anne Long, Valerie Anderson, Natalie

Diggins, Zan Nix, Faith Graham, Katharina Schütze, Lisa Donoughe, Dan Jamison and Denis Oakley. Conversations with Anne Bartlett at the inception stage of writing brought into focus my underlying motivation for the project, and affirmed at the end that I'd found my mark.

Kristin Hatcher understands that writing as a sole endeavor is tough, so she formed Writing in Community within Seth Godin's Akimbo network. There I could be in authoring cahoots with Angus Lockyer, Michael Cohen, Michael McCue, Heather Button, Louise Karch, Kerry Itami, David Bourne, Geoff Saab, Tara Russell, Susan Fritz, Michele Stanners, Rebecca Schalm, Paul Karvanis, Annie Keeling, Debbie Moller, Laurie Riedman, Annie Keeling, Russell John, Diane Osgood, Cindy Villanueva, Susan Walter, Laurie Riedman, Deb Brown Maher, Melissa Kalinowski, Luke Harris, Karen Collins and Annette Mason. Morning online writing dates with Tonya Cole and Toku McCree kept the fire stoked, while weekly calls with a subgroup we dubbed the Writers Salon— Julie Rains, Lynn Carnes, Katy Dalgleish, Kym Dakin-Neal, and Terri Tomoff—illuminated things, big and tiny, about getting our words down and our works shipped.

Without Bernadette Jiwa and her elegant Story Skills Workshop, the personal accounts on these pages might never have risen to life. It was a privilege to learn—and coach—the craft alongside Bernadette, Mark Dyck, Tom Huntington, Luke Harris, Anne Roche, Cat Preston, Heather Chavin, Conor McCarthy, Paula Braun, Nadine Kelly, Victoria Hefty, Mandell Conway and Enrika Greathouse.

Many fellow meditators contributed mightily to my

evolution as a human and an author. The turns my life took might have been quite different had it not been for Linda, David, Jen, Anu, Sophia and Wenndi.

Editorial coaching from Andra Miller, Rachel Small, Sharon Littrell, and Isabel Kuh consistently improved the structure, content and flow of Winnowing, while Jule Kucera's design tips led me to Damonza, a boutique firm that captured the essence of the book for both the cover design and interior layout. Brooks Becker provided thoughtful proofreading in the final stage. As the pieces of the book started coming together, I used AI to evaluate prose and address grammar before passing the manuscript to my professional editors and proofreader.

Deciding to independently publish required learning new skills. Jane Friedman's webinars were a lifeline, along with Becky Robinson's book *Reach*. On the promotional side, Michael Feeley taught me how to directly and bravely seek endorsements, while Rick Katagawa and Wilson Silva made sure any marketing copy spoke squarely to readers. The brilliant teachings of Robert and Rosalind Fritz meant the entire project was dynamized with structural tension.

When my siblings and I were kids, our parents told us that we could be anything we wanted. I'm glad they broadcasted it. One could say it's not technically accurate, but what they taught us was to challenge arbitrary limits, whether they came from within or without. Without them, none of this would have happened. Mom (an English teacher beloved by her students) read each bit of the book as it emerged and offered meticulously refined grammar and punctuation suggestions along with endless encouragement.

Last but not least, the man who chose St. Honoré for our first date consistently displays respect and quiet generosity each time I disappear, whether to write or meditate. I'm grateful that his love language speaks in this way.

A SMALL REQUEST

If you enjoyed *Winnowing*, please consider leaving a review on Amazon and Goodreads. Even if what you write is brief and left anonymously, it can make the book more discoverable to future readers.

Thanks for your support.

Kira

Kira Higgs is a facilitative strategist, structural consultant, published writer and active athlete. Raised in New England in the Christian tradition, Kira migrated to meditation, and it became the bedrock of her spiritual practice. She calls the West Coast home and travels to beautiful countrysides to enjoy the world from the seat of a bicycle. *Winnowing* is her debut book.

www.ingramcontent.com/pod-product-compliance
Lightning Source LLC
Chambersburg PA
CBHW051307130726
47987CB00004B/1700